A
LOEB
CLASSICAL
LIBRARY
READER

HARVARD UNIVERSITY PRESS
CAMBRIDGE, MASSACHUSETTS
LONDON, ENGLAND

Library of Congress Catalog Card Number 2005052600
CIP data available from the Library of Congress

ISBN 0-674-99616-X

Printed in the United States of America

CONTENTS

CONTENTS

PREFACE

This selection of lapidary nuggets drawn from thirty-three of antiquity's major authors includes poetry, dialogue, philosophical writing, history, descriptive reporting, satire, and fiction—giving a glimpse at the wide range of arts and sciences, styles and convictions, of Greco-Roman culture.

The selections span twelve centuries, from Homer to Saint Jerome. They are given in two sequences in roughly chronological order, the Greeks first, followed by the Romans. The texts and translations are reproduced as they appear in Loeb volumes; footnotes have been reduced in keeping with the needs of this compact sampling. An index to the passages is at the end.

The Loeb Classical Library is the only existing series of books which, through original text and facing English translation, gives access to all that is important in Greek and Latin literature. This reader can do no more than represent a small portion of the riches in that treasury. A complete list of works in the Loeb Classical Library is available from Harvard University Press and at www.hup.harvard.edu/loeb.

HOMER

Translation by A. T. Murray;
revised by George E. Dimock

"ἦμος δ' ἠριγένεια φάνη ῥοδοδάκτυλος Ἠώς,
καὶ τότε πῦρ ἀνέκαιε καὶ ἤμελγε κλυτὰ μῆλα,
πάντα κατὰ μοῖραν, καὶ ὑπ' ἔμβρυον ἧκεν ἑκάστῃ.
310 αὐτὰρ ἐπεὶ δὴ σπεῦσε πονησάμενος τὰ ἃ ἔργα,
σὺν δ' ὅ γε δὴ αὖτε δύω μάρψας ὡπλίσσατο δεῖπνον.
δειπνήσας δ' ἄντρου ἐξήλασε πίονα μῆλα,
ῥηιδίως ἀφελὼν θυρεὸν μέγαν· αὐτὰρ ἔπειτα
ἂψ ἐπέθηχ', ὡς εἴ τε φαρέτρῃ πῶμ' ἐπιθείη.
315 πολλῇ δὲ ῥοίζῳ πρὸς ὄρος τρέπε πίονα μῆλα
Κύκλωψ· αὐτὰρ ἐγὼ λιπόμην κακὰ βυσσοδομεύων,
εἴ πως τισαίμην, δοίη δέ μοι εὖχος Ἀθήνη.
     "ἥδε δέ μοι κατὰ θυμὸν ἀρίστη φαίνετο βουλή.
Κύκλωπος γὰρ ἔκειτο μέγα ῥόπαλον παρὰ σηκῷ,
320 χλωρὸν ἐλαΐνεον· τὸ μὲν ἔκταμεν, ὄφρα φοροίη
αὐανθέν. τὸ μὲν ἄμμες ἐΐσκομεν εἰσορόωντες
ὅσσον θ' ἱστὸν νηὸς ἐεικοσόροιο μελαίνης,
φορτίδος εὐρείης, ἥ τ' ἐκπεράᾳ μέγα λαῖτμα·
τόσσον ἔην μῆκος, τόσσον πάχος εἰσοράασθαι.

2

Odyssey 9.307–414

Odysseus describes how he tricked the Cyclops
in order to escape from the giant's cave

"As soon as early Dawn appeared, the rosy-fingered, he[1]
rekindled the fire and milked his fine flocks all in turn, and
beneath each dam placed her young. Then, when he had
busily performed his tasks, again he seized two men to-
gether and made ready his meal. And when he had made
his meal he drove his fat flocks forth from the cave, easily
moving away the great doorstone; and then he put it in
place again, as one might set the lid upon a quiver. Then
with loud whistling the Cyclops turned his fat flocks to-
ward the mountain, and I was left there, devising evil in the
depths of my heart, if in any way I might take vengeance on
him, and Athene grant me glory.

"Now this seemed to my mind the best plan. There lay
beside a sheep pen a great club of the Cyclops, a staff of
green olivewood, which he had cut to carry with him when
dry; and as we looked at it we thought it as large as is the
mast of a black ship of twenty oars, a merchantman, broad
of beam, which crosses over the great gulf; so huge it was in
length, so huge in breadth to look upon. Going up to it, I

[1] Cyclops. The men he eats are Odysseus' comrades.

3

325 τοῦ μὲν ὅσον τ᾽ ὄργυιαν ἐγὼν ἀπέκοψα παραστὰς
καὶ παρέθηχ᾽ ἑτάροισιν, ἀποξῦναι δ᾽ ἐκέλευσα·
οἱ δ᾽ ὁμαλὸν ποίησαν· ἐγὼ δ᾽ ἐθόωσα παραστὰς
ἄκρον, ἄφαρ δὲ λαβὼν ἐπυράκτεον ἐν πυρὶ κηλέῳ.
καὶ τὸ μὲν εὖ κατέθηκα κατακρύψας ὑπὸ κόπρῳ,
330 ἥ ῥα κατὰ σπείους κέχυτο μεγάλ᾽ ἤλιθα πολλή·
αὐτὰρ τοὺς ἄλλους κλήρῳ πεπαλάσθαι ἄνωγον,
ὅς τις τολμήσειεν ἐμοὶ σὺν μοχλὸν ἀείρας
τρῖψαι ἐν ὀφθαλμῷ, ὅτε τὸν γλυκὺς ὕπνος ἱκάνοι.
οἱ δ᾽ ἔλαχον τοὺς ἄν κε καὶ ἤθελον αὐτὸς ἑλέσθαι,
335 τέσσαρες, αὐτὰρ ἐγὼ πέμπτος μετὰ τοῖσιν ἐλέγμην.
ἑσπέριος δ᾽ ἦλθεν καλλίτριχα μῆλα νομεύων.
αὐτίκα δ᾽ εἰς εὐρὺ σπέος ἤλασε πίονα μῆλα
πάντα μάλ᾽, οὐδέ τι λεῖπε βαθείης ἔκτοθεν αὐλῆς,
ἤ τι ὀισάμενος, ἢ καὶ θεὸς ὣς ἐκέλευσεν.
340 αὐτὰρ ἔπειτ᾽ ἐπέθηκε θυρεὸν μέγαν ὑψόσ᾽ ἀείρας,
ἑζόμενος δ᾽ ἤμελγεν ὄις καὶ μηκάδας αἶγας,
πάντα κατὰ μοῖραν, καὶ ὑπ᾽ ἔμβρυον ἧκεν ἑκάστῃ.
αὐτὰρ ἐπεὶ δὴ σπεῦσε πονησάμενος τὰ ἃ ἔργα,
σὺν δ᾽ ὅ γε δὴ αὖτε δύω μάρψας ὡπλίσσατο δόρπον.
345 καὶ τότ᾽ ἐγὼ Κύκλωπα προσηύδων ἄγχι παραστάς,
κισσύβιον μετὰ χερσὶν ἔχων μέλανος οἴνοιο·

"Κύκλωψ, τῆ, πίε οἶνον, ἐπεὶ φάγες ἀνδρόμεα κρέα,
ὄφρ᾽ εἰδῇς οἷόν τι ποτὸν τόδε νηῦς ἐκεκεύθει
ἡμετέρη. σοὶ δ᾽ αὖ λοιβὴν φέρον, εἴ μ᾽ ἐλεήσας
350 οἴκαδε πέμψειας· σὺ δὲ μαίνεαι οὐκέτ᾽ ἀνεκτῶς.
σχέτλιε, πῶς κέν τίς σε καὶ ὕστερον ἄλλος ἵκοιτο
ἀνθρώπων πολέων, ἐπεὶ οὐ κατὰ μοῖραν ἔρεξας;

cut off about a fathom's length and handed it to my comrades, bidding them dress it down; and they made it smooth, and I, standing by, sharpened it at the point, and then took it at once and hardened it in the blazing fire. Then I laid it carefully away, hiding it beneath the dung, which lay in great heaps about the cave. And I told the others to cast lots among them, which of them should have the hardihood with me to lift the stake and grind it into his eye when sweet sleep should come upon him. And the lot fell upon those whom I myself would have wished to choose; four they were, and I was numbered with them as the fifth. At evening he came, herding his fine-fleeced sheep. Without delay he drove into the wide cave his fat flocks one and all, and left not one outside in the deep courtyard, either from some foreboding or because a god so bade him. Then he lifted up and set in place the great doorstone, and sitting down he milked the ewes and bleating goats all in turn, and beneath each dam he placed her young. But when he had busily performed his tasks, again he seized two men together and made ready his supper. Then I drew near and spoke to the Cyclops, holding in my hands an ivy-wood bowl of dark wine:

"'Cyclops, here; drink wine, now that you have had your meal of human flesh, that you may know what kind of drink this is which our ship contained. It was to you that I was bringing it as a drink offering, in the hope that, touched with pity, you might send me on my way home; but you rage in a way that is past all bearing. Cruel man, how shall anyone of all the men there are ever come to you again hereafter, since what you have done is not right?'

"ὣς ἐφάμην, ὁ δ' ἔδεκτο καὶ ἔκπιεν· ἥσατο δ' αἰνῶς
ἡδὺ ποτὸν πίνων καί μ' ᾔτεε δεύτερον αὖτις·

355 "'δός μοι ἔτι πρόφρων, καί μοι τεὸν οὔνομα εἰπὲ
αὐτίκα νῦν, ἵνα τοι δῶ ξείνιον, ᾧ κε σὺ χαίρῃς·
καὶ γὰρ Κυκλώπεσσι φέρει ζείδωρος ἄρουρα
οἶνον ἐρισταφύλον, καί σφιν Διὸς ὄμβρος ἀέξει·
ἀλλὰ τόδ' ἀμβροσίης καὶ νέκταρός ἐστιν ἀπορρώξ.'

360 "ὣς φάτ', ἀτάρ οἱ αὖτις ἐγὼ πόρον αἴθοπα οἶνον.
τρὶς μὲν ἔδωκα φέρων, τρὶς δ' ἔκπιεν ἀφραδίῃσιν.
αὐτὰρ ἐπεὶ Κύκλωπα περὶ φρένας ἤλυθεν οἶνος,
καὶ τότε δή μιν ἔπεσσι προσηύδων μειλιχίοισι·

"'Κύκλωψ, εἰρωτᾷς μ' ὄνομα κλυτόν, αὐτὰρ ἐγώ τοι
365 ἐξερέω· σὺ δέ μοι δὸς ξείνιον, ὥς περ ὑπέστης.
Οὖτις ἐμοί γ' ὄνομα· Οὖτιν δέ με κικλήσκουσι
μήτηρ ἠδὲ πατὴρ ἠδ' ἄλλοι πάντες ἑταῖροι.'

"ὣς ἐφάμην, ὁ δέ μ' αὐτίκ' ἀμείβετο νηλέι θυμῷ·
Ὦτιν ἐγὼ πύματον ἔδομαι μετὰ οἷς ἑτάροισιν,
370 τοὺς δ' ἄλλους πρόσθεν· τὸ δέ τοι ξεινήιον ἔσται.'

"ἦ καὶ ἀνακλινθεὶς πέσεν ὕπτιος, αὐτὰρ ἔπειτα
κεῖτ' ἀποδοχμώσας παχὺν αὐχένα, κὰδ δέ μιν ὕπνος
ᾕρει πανδαμάτωρ· φάρυγος δ' ἐξέσσυτο οἶνος
ψωμοί τ' ἀνδρόμεοι· ὁ δ' ἐρεύγετο οἰνοβαρείων.

375 καὶ τότ' ἐγὼ τὸν μοχλὸν ὑπὸ σποδοῦ ἤλασα πολλῆς,
ἧος θερμαίνοιτο· ἔπεσσι δὲ πάντας ἑταίρους
θάρσυνον, μή τίς μοι ὑποδείσας ἀναδύη.
ἀλλ' ὅτε δὴ τάχ' ὁ μοχλὸς ἐλάινος ἐν πυρὶ μέλλεν
ἅψεσθαι, χλωρός περ ἐών, διεφαίνετο δ' αἰνῶς,
380 καὶ τότ' ἐγὼν ἆσσον φέρον ἐκ πυρός, ἀμφὶ δ' ἑταῖροι

6

"So I spoke, and he took the cup and drained it, and was wondrously pleased as he drank the sweet draught, and asked me for it again a second time:

"'Give me it again with a ready heart, and tell me your name at once, that I may give you a stranger's gift at which you may be glad. For among the Cyclopes the earth, the giver of grain, bears the rich clusters of wine, and the rain of Zeus gives them increase; but this is a draught from a stream of ambrosia and nectar.'

"So he spoke, and again I handed him the sparkling wine. Three times I brought and gave it to him, and three times he drained it in his folly. But when the wine had got round the wits of the Cyclops, then I spoke to him with winning words:

"'Cyclops, you ask me of my glorious name, and I will tell you it; and do you give me a stranger's gift, even as you promised. Nobody is my name, Nobody they call me—my mother and my father, and all my comrades as well.'

"So I spoke, and at once he answered me with pitiless heart: 'Nobody will I eat last among his comrades, and the others before him; this shall be your gift.'

"He spoke, and reeling fell upon his back, and lay there with his thick neck bent aslant, and sleep that conquers all laid hold on him. And from his gullet came forth wine and bits of human flesh, and he vomited in his drunken sleep. Then it was I who thrust the stake under the deep ashes until it should grow hot, and heartened all my comrades with cheering words, so that no man might falter from fear. But when presently that stake of olivewood was about to catch fire, green though it was, and began to glow terribly, then it was I who brought it near from the fire, and my

HOMER

ἵσταντ'· αὐτὰρ θάρσος ἐνέπνευσεν μέγα δαίμων.
οἱ μὲν μοχλὸν ἑλόντες ἐλάινον, ὀξὺν ἐπ' ἄκρῳ,
ὀφθαλμῷ ἐνέρεισαν· ἐγὼ δ' ἐφύπερθεν ἐρεισθεὶς
δίνεον, ὡς ὅτε τις τρυπῷ δόρυ νήιον ἀνὴρ
385 τρυπάνῳ, οἱ δέ τ' ἔνερθεν ὑποσσείουσιν ἱμάντι
ἁψάμενοι ἑκάτερθε, τὸ δὲ τρέχει ἐμμενὲς αἰεί.
ὣς τοῦ ἐν ὀφθαλμῷ πυριήκεα μοχλὸν ἑλόντες
δινέομεν, τὸν δ' αἷμα περίρρεε θερμὸν ἐόντα.
πάντα δέ οἱ βλέφαρ' ἀμφὶ καὶ ὀφρύας εὖσεν ἀυτμὴ
390 γλήνης καιομένης, σφαραγεῦντο δέ οἱ πυρὶ ῥίζαι.
ὡς δ' ὅτ' ἀνὴρ χαλκεὺς πέλεκυν μέγαν ἠὲ σκέπαρνον
εἰν ὕδατι ψυχρῷ βάπτῃ μεγάλα ἰάχοντα
φαρμάσσων· τὸ γὰρ αὖτε σιδήρου γε κράτος ἐστίν·
ὣς τοῦ σίζ' ὀφθαλμὸς ἐλαϊνέῳ περὶ μοχλῷ.
395 σμερδαλέον δὲ μέγ' ᾤμωξεν, περὶ δ' ἴαχε πέτρη,
ἡμεῖς δὲ δείσαντες ἀπεσσύμεθ'· αὐτὰρ ὁ μοχλὸν
ἐξέρυσ' ὀφθαλμοῖο πεφυρμένον αἵματι πολλῷ.
τὸν μὲν ἔπειτ' ἔρριψεν ἀπὸ ἕο χερσὶν ἀλύων,
αὐτὰρ ὁ Κύκλωπας μεγάλ' ἤπυεν, οἵ ῥά μιν ἀμφὶς
400 ᾤκεον ἐν σπήεσσι δι' ἄκριας ἠνεμοέσσας.
οἱ δὲ βοῆς ἀίοντες ἐφοίτων ἄλλοθεν ἄλλος,
ἱστάμενοι δ' εἴροντο περὶ σπέος ὅττι ἑ κήδοι·
    "'τίπτε τόσον, Πολύφημ', ἀρημένος ὧδ' ἐβόησας
νύκτα δι' ἀμβροσίην καὶ ἀύπνους ἄμμε τίθησθα;
405 ἦ μή τίς σευ μῆλα βροτῶν ἀέκοντος ἐλαύνει;
ἦ μή τίς σ' αὐτὸν κτείνει δόλῳ ἠὲ βίηφιν;'
    "τοὺς δ' αὖτ' ἐξ ἄντρου προσέφη κρατερὸς
        Πολύφημος·

8

comrades stood round me and a god breathed into us great courage. They took the stake of olivewood, sharp at the point, and thrust it into his eye, while I, throwing my weight upon it from above, whirled it round, as a man bores a ship's timber with a drill, while those below keep it spinning with the strap, which they lay hold of by either end, and the drill runs unceasingly. Even so we took the fiery-pointed stake and whirled it around in his eye, and the blood flowed round it, all hot as it was. His eyelids above and below and his brows were all singed by the flame from the burning eyeball, and its roots crackled in the fire. And as when a smith dips a great axe or an adze in cold water to temper it and it makes a great hissing—for from this comes the strength of iron—so did his eye hiss round the stake of olivewood. Terribly then did he cry aloud, and the rock rang around; and we, seized with terror, shrank back, while he wrenched from his eye the stake, all befouled with blood. Then with both arms he flung it from him, beside himself, and shouted to the Cyclopes, who dwelt round about him in caves among the windy heights, and they heard his cry and came thronging from every side, and standing around the cave asked him what ailed him:

"'What sore distress is this, Polyphemus, that you cry out thus through the immortal night, and make us sleepless? Can it be that some mortal man is driving off your flocks against your will, or killing you yourself by guile or by strength?'

"Then from inside the cave strong Polyphemus

'ὦ φίλοι, Οὖτίς με κτείνει δόλῳ οὐδὲ βίηφιν.'

"οἱ δ᾽ ἀπαμειβόμενοι ἔπεα πτερόεντ᾽ ἀγόρευον·

410 'εἰ μὲν δὴ μή τίς σε βιάζεται οἶον ἐόντα,

νοῦσον γ᾽ οὔ πως ἔστι Διὸς μεγάλου ἀλέασθαι,

ἀλλὰ σύ γ᾽ εὔχεο πατρὶ Ποσειδάωνι ἄνακτι.'

"ὣς ἄρ᾽ ἔφαν ἀπιόντες, ἐμὸν δ᾽ ἐγέλασσε φίλον κῆρ,

ὡς ὄνομ᾽ ἐξαπάτησεν ἐμὸν καὶ μῆτις ἀμύμων."

answered them: 'My friends, it is Nobody that is slaying me by guile and not by force.'

"And they made answer and addressed him with winged words: 'If, then, nobody does violence to you all alone as you are, sickness which comes from Zeus there is no way you can escape; you must pray to our father the lord Poseidon.'

"So they spoke and went their way; and my heart laughed within me that my name and flawless scheme had so beguiled."

HESIOD

Translation by Glenn W. Most

Κρύψαντες γὰρ ἔχουσι θεοὶ βίον ἀνθρώποισιν.
ῥηιδίως γάρ κεν καὶ ἐπ᾽ ἤματι ἐργάσσαιο,
ὥστε σε κεῖς ἐνιαυτὸν ἔχειν καὶ ἀεργὸν ἐόντα·
45 αἶψά κε πηδάλιον μὲν ὑπὲρ καπνοῦ καταθεῖο,
ἔργα βοῶν δ᾽ ἀπόλοιτο καὶ ἡμιόνων ταλαεργῶν.
ἀλλὰ Ζεὺς ἔκρυψε χολωσάμενος φρεσὶ ᾗσιν,
ὅττι μιν ἐξαπάτησε Προμηθεὺς ἀγκυλομήτης·
τοὔνεκ᾽ ἄρ᾽ ἀνθρώποισιν ἐμήσατο κήδεα λυγρά,
50 κρύψε δὲ πῦρ· τὸ μὲν αὖτις ἐὺς πάις Ἰαπετοῖο
ἔκλεψ᾽ ἀνθρώποισι Διὸς παρὰ μητιόεντος
ἐν κοίλῳ νάρθηκι, λαθὼν Δία τερπικέραυνον.
τὸν δὲ χολωσάμενος προσέφη νεφεληγερέτα Ζεύς·
"Ἰαπετιονίδη, πάντων πέρι μήδεα εἰδώς,
55 χαίρεις πῦρ κλέψας καὶ ἐμὰς φρένας ἠπεροπεύσας,
σοί τ᾽ αὐτῷ μέγα πῆμα καὶ ἀνδράσιν ἐσσομένοισιν.
τοῖς δ᾽ ἐγὼ ἀντὶ πυρὸς δώσω κακόν, ᾧ κεν ἅπαντες

Works and Days 42–105

Angry that humans have acquired (through Prometheus)
the gift of fire, Zeus devises retribution, creating the
first woman, cause of mortals' hardships

For the gods keep the means of life concealed from humans. Otherwise you would easily be able to work in just one day so as to have enough for a whole year even without working; and quickly you would store the rudder above the smoke, and the work of the cattle and of the hard-working mules would be ended.

But Zeus concealed it, angry in his heart because crooked-counseled Prometheus (Forethought) had deceived him. For that reason, then, he devised baneful evils for humans, and he concealed fire; but the good son of Iapetus[1] stole it back from the counselor Zeus in a hollow fennel stalk for humans, escaping the notice of Zeus who delights in the thunderbolt.

And the cloud-gatherer Zeus spoke to him in anger: "Son of Iapetus, you who know counsels beyond all others, you are pleased that you have stolen fire and beguiled my mind—a great grief for you yourself, and for men to come. To them I shall give in exchange for fire an evil in which

[1] Prometheus.

13

τέρπωνται κατὰ θυμὸν ἑὸν κακὸν ἀμφαγαπῶντες."

Ὣς ἔφατ', ἐκ δ' ἐγέλασσε πατὴρ ἀνδρῶν τε θεῶν τε·

60 Ἥφαιστον δ' ἐκέλευσε περικλυτὸν ὅττι τάχιστα
γαῖαν ὕδει φύρειν, ἐν δ' ἀνθρώπου θέμεν αὐδὴν
καὶ σθένος, ἀθανάτῃς δὲ θεῇς εἰς ὦπα ἐΐσκειν
παρθενικῆς καλὸν εἶδος ἐπήρατον· αὐτὰρ Ἀθήνην
ἔργα διδασκῆσαι, πολυδαίδαλον ἱστὸν ὑφαίνειν·

65 καὶ χάριν ἀμφιχέαι κεφαλῇ χρυσέην Ἀφροδίτην
καὶ πόθον ἀργαλέον καὶ γυιοβόρους μελεδώνας·
ἐν δὲ θέμεν κύνεόν τε νόον καὶ ἐπίκλοπον ἦθος
Ἑρμείην ἤνωγε, διάκτορον Ἀργεϊφόντην.

Ὣς ἔφαθ', οἳ δ' ἐπίθοντο Διὶ Κρονίωνι ἄνακτι.

70 αὐτίκα δ' ἐκ γαίης πλάσσε κλυτὸς Ἀμφιγυήεις
παρθένῳ αἰδοίῃ ἴκελον Κρονίδεω διὰ βουλάς·
ζῶσε δὲ καὶ κόσμησε θεὰ γλαυκῶπις Ἀθήνη·
ἀμφὶ δέ οἱ Χάριτές τε θεαὶ καὶ πότνια Πειθὼ
ὅρμους χρυσείους ἔθεσαν χροΐ· ἀμφὶ δὲ τήν γε

75 Ὧραι καλλίκομοι στέφον ἄνθεσι εἰαρινοῖσιν·
πάντα δέ οἱ χροΐ κόσμον ἐφήρμοσε Παλλὰς
    Ἀθήνη·
ἐν δ' ἄρα οἱ στήθεσσι διάκτορος Ἀργεϊφόντης
ψεύδεά θ' αἱμυλίους τε λόγους καὶ ἐπίκλοπον ἦθος
τεῦξε Διὸς βουλῇσι βαρυκτύπου· ἐν δ' ἄρα φωνὴν

80 θῆκε θεῶν κῆρυξ, ὀνόμηνε δὲ τήνδε γυναῖκα
Πανδώρην, ὅτι πάντες Ὀλύμπια δώματ' ἔχοντες
δῶρον ἐδώρησαν, πῆμ' ἀνδράσιν ἀλφηστῇσιν.

Αὐτὰρ ἐπεὶ δόλον αἰπὺν ἀμήχανον ἐξετέλεσσεν,
εἰς Ἐπιμηθέα πέμπε πατὴρ κλυτὸν Ἀργεϊφόντην

14

they may all take pleasure in their spirit, embracing their own evil."

So he spoke, and he laughed out loud, the father of men and of gods. He commanded renowned Hephaestus to mix earth with water as quickly as possible, and to put into it the voice and strength of a human, and to make her similar in her face to the deathless goddesses, a beautiful, lovely form of a maiden. And he told Athena to teach her crafts, to weave richly worked cloth; and golden Aphrodite to shed around her head grace and painful desire and limb-devouring cares; and he ordered Hermes, the intermediary, the killer of Argus, to put into her a dog's mind and a thievish character.

So he spoke, and they obeyed Zeus, the lord, Cronus' son. Immediately the famous Lame One fabricated out of earth a likeness of a modest maiden, by the plans of Cronus' son; and the goddess, bright-eyed Athena, gave her a girdle and ornaments; and the goddesses Graces and queenly Persuasion placed golden chains all around on her body; and the beautiful-haired Seasons crowned her all around with spring flowers; and Pallas Athena fitted the whole ornamentation to her body. Then into her breast the intermediary, the killer of Argus, set lies and guileful words and a thievish character, by the plans of deep-thundering Zeus; and the messenger of the gods placed a voice in her and named this woman Pandora (All-gift), since all those who have their mansions on Olympus had given her a gift—a woe for men who live on bread.

But when he had completed the sheer deception, past help, the father sent the famous killer of Argus, the swift

85 δῶρον ἄγοντα, θεῶν ταχὺν ἄγγελον· οὐδ᾽
    Ἐπιμηθεὺς
ἐφράσαθ᾽ ὥς οἱ ἔειπε Προμηθεὺς μή ποτε δῶρον
δέξασθαι πὰρ Ζηνὸς Ὀλυμπίου, ἀλλ᾽ ἀποπέμπειν
ἐξοπίσω, μή πού τι κακὸν θνητοῖσι γένηται·
αὐτὰρ ὁ δεξάμενος, ὅτε δὴ κακὸν εἶχ᾽, ἐνόησε.
90   Πρὶν μὲν γὰρ ζώεσκον ἐπὶ χθονὶ φῦλ᾽ ἀνθρώπων
νόσφιν ἄτερ τε κακῶν καὶ ἄτερ χαλεποῖο πόνοιο
νούσων τ᾽ ἀργαλέων, αἵ τ᾽ ἀνδράσι κῆρας ἔδωκαν.
[αἶψα γὰρ ἐν κακότητι βροτοὶ καταγηράσκουσιν.]
ἀλλὰ γυνὴ χείρεσσι πίθου μέγα πῶμ᾽ ἀφελοῦσα
95 ἐσκέδασ᾽, ἀνθρώποισι δ᾽ ἐμήσατο κήδεα λυγρά.
μούνη δ᾽ αὐτόθι Ἐλπὶς ἐν ἀρρήκτοισι δόμοισιν
ἔνδον ἔμεινε πίθου ὑπὸ χείλεσιν οὐδὲ θύραζε
ἐξέπτη· πρόσθεν γὰρ ἐπέμβαλε πῶμα πίθοιο
αἰγιόχου βουλῇσι Διὸς νεφεληγερέταο.
100 ἄλλα δὲ μυρία λυγρὰ κατ᾽ ἀνθρώπους ἀλάληται·
πλείη μὲν γὰρ γαῖα κακῶν, πλείη δὲ θάλασσα·
νοῦσοι δ᾽ ἀνθρώποισιν ἐφ᾽ ἡμέρῃ, αἱ δ᾽ ἐπὶ νυκτὶ
αὐτόματοι φοιτῶσι κακὰ θνητοῖσι φέρουσαι
σιγῇ, ἐπεὶ φωνὴν ἐξείλετο μητίετα Ζεύς.
105 οὕτως οὔ τί πη ἔστι Διὸς νόον ἐξαλέασθαι.

messenger of the gods, to take her as a gift to Epimetheus (Afterthought). And Epimetheus did not consider that Prometheus had told him never to accept a gift from Olympian Zeus, but to send it back again, lest something evil happen to mortals; but it was only after he accepted her, when he already had the evil, that he understood.

For previously the tribes of men used to live upon the earth entirely apart from evils, and without grievous toil and distressful diseases, which give death to men. [For in misery mortals grow old at once.][2] But the woman removed the great lid from the storage jar with her hands and scattered all its contents abroad, and so wrought baneful evils for humans. Only Anticipation[3] remained there in its unbreakable home under the mouth of the storage jar, and did not fly out; for before that could happen she closed the lid of the storage jar, by the plans of the aegis-holder, the cloud-gatherer, Zeus. But countless other miseries roam among mankind; for the earth is full of evils, and the sea is full; and some sicknesses come upon men by day, and others by night, of their own accord, bearing evils to mortals in silence, since the counselor Zeus took their voice away. Thus it is not possible in any way to evade the mind of Zeus.

[2] This line is found in the margin or text of very few manuscripts; it is identical with *Od.* 19.360 and is generally rejected here as an intrusive gloss.

[3] Often translated "Hope"; but the Greek word can mean anticipation of bad as well as of good things.

PINDAR

Translation by William H. Race

Γ΄ ὁ δ' ἄρ' ἐν Πίσᾳ ἕλσαις ὅλον τε στρατόν
λᾴαν τε πᾶσαν Διὸς ἄλκιμος
45 υἱὸς σταθμᾶτο ζάθεον ἄλσος πατρὶ μεγίστῳ·
    περὶ δὲ πάξαις Ἄλτιν μὲν ὅγ' ἐν καθαρῷ
    διέκρινε, τὸ δὲ κύκλῳ πέδον
    ἔθηκε δόρπου λύσιν,
    τιμάσαις πόρον Ἀλφεοῦ
    μετὰ δώδεκ' ἀνάκτων θεῶν· καὶ πάγον

50 Κρόνου προσεφθέγξατο· πρόσθε γὰρ
    νώνυμνος, ἇς Οἰνόμαος ἆρχε, βρέχετο πολλᾷ
      νιφάδι. ταύτᾳ δ' ἐν πρωτογόνῳ τελετᾷ
    παρέσταν μὲν ἄρα Μοῖραι σχεδόν
    ὅ τ' ἐξελέγχων μόνος
    ἀλάθειαν ἐτήτυμον

55 Χρόνος. τὸ δὲ σαφανὲς ἰὼν πόρσω κατέφρασεν,
    ὁπᾷ τὰν πολέμοιο δόσιν

18

Olympian Odes 10.43–106

The first Olympic games, founded by Herakles

Thereupon, Zeus' valiant son[1] gathered the entire army   Str. 3
and all the booty at Pisa,
and measured out a sacred precinct for his father   45
    most mighty. He fenced in the Altis and set it apart
in the open, and he made the surrounding plain
a resting place for banqueting,
and honored the stream of Alpheos

along with the twelve ruling gods. And he gave the hill   Ant. 3
of Kronos its name, because before that it had none,   50
when, during Oinomaos' reign, it was drenched
    with much snow. And at that founding ceremony
the Fates stood near at hand,
as did the sole assayer
of genuine truth,

Time, which in its onward march clearly revealed   Ep. 3
how Herakles divided up that gift of war[2]   56

[1] Herakles.
[2] The booty he had taken from destroying Augeas' city (44).

19

ἀκρόθινα διελὼν ἔθυε καὶ
   πενταετηρίδ᾽ ὅπως ἄρα
ἔστασεν ἑορτὰν σὺν Ὀλυμπιάδι πρώτᾳ
νικαφορίαισί τε.
60 τίς δὴ ποταίνιον
ἔλαχε στέφανον
χείρεσσι ποσίν τε καὶ ἅρματι,
ἀγώνιον ἐν δόξᾳ θέμενος
   εὖχος, ἔργῳ καθελών;

Δ΄ στάδιον μὲν ἀρίστευσεν, εὐθὺν τόνον
65 ποσσὶ τρέχων, παῖς ὁ Λικυμνίου
Οἰωνός· ἷκεν δὲ Μιδέαθεν στρατὸν ἐλαύνων·
   ὁ δὲ πάλᾳ κυδαίνων Ἔχεμος Τεγέαν·
Δόρυκλος δ᾽ ἔφερε πυγμᾶς τέλος,
Τίρυνθα ναίων πόλιν·
ἀν᾽ ἵπποισι δὲ τέτρασιν

70 ἀπὸ Μαντινέας Σᾶμος ὁ Ἁλιροθίου·
ἄκοντι Φράστωρ ἔλασε σκοπόν·
μᾶκος δὲ Νικεὺς ἔδικε πέτρῳ χέρα κυκλώσαις
   ὑπὲρ ἁπάντων, καὶ συμμαχία θόρυβον
παραίθυξε μέγαν. ἐν δ᾽ ἕσπερον
ἔφλεξεν εὐώπιδος
75 σελάνας ἐρατὸν φάος.

and offered up its best portion,
    and how he then founded
the quadrennial festival with the first Olympiad
and its victories.
Who then won   60
the new crown
with hands or feet or with chariot,
after fixing in his thoughts a triumph
    in the contest and achieving it in deed?

The winner of the stadion, as he ran the straight stretch   Str. 4
with his feet, was Likymnios' son,   65
Oionos, who came at the head of his army from Midea.
    In the wrestling Echemos gained glory for Tegea.
Doryklos won the prize in boxing,
who lived in the city of Tiryns,
and in the four-horse chariot race

it was Samos of Mantinea, son of Halirothios.   Ant. 4
Phrastor hit the mark with the javelin,   71
while with a swing of his hand Nikeus cast the stone[3]
    a distance beyond all others, and his fellow soldiers
let fly a great cheer. Then the lovely light
of the moon's beautiful face
lit up the evening,   75

---

[3] The early discuses were made of stone, and accuracy rather than distance was required in the javelin throw. Eventually these two events were incorporated into the pentathlon (cf. *Isth.* 1.24–27).

PINDAR

ἀείδετο δὲ πὰν τέμενος τερπναῖσι θαλίαις
τὸν ἐγκώμιον ἀμφὶ τρόπον.
ἀρχαῖς δὲ προτέραις ἑπόμενοι
 καί νυν ἐπωνυμίαν χάριν
νίκας ἀγερώχου κελαδησόμεθα βροντάν
80 καὶ πυρπάλαμον βέλος
ὀρσικτύπου Διός,
ἐν ἅπαντι κράτει
αἴθωνα κεραυνὸν ἀραρότα·
χλιδῶσα δὲ μολπὰ πρὸς κάλαμον
 ἀντιάξει μελέων,

Ε΄ τὰ παρ' εὐκλέι Δίρκᾳ χρόνῳ μὲν φάνεν·
86 ἀλλ' ὥτε παῖς ἐξ ἀλόχου πατρί
ποθεινὸς ἵκοντι νεότατος τὸ πάλιν ἤδη,
 μάλα δέ οἱ θερμαίνει φιλότατι νόον·
ἐπεὶ πλοῦτος ὁ λαχὼν ποιμένα
ἐπακτὸν ἀλλότριον
90 θνᾴσκοντι στυγερώτατος·

καὶ ὅταν καλὰ ἔρξαις ἀοιδᾶς ἄτερ,
Ἀγησίδαμ', εἰς Ἀίδα σταθμόν
ἀνὴρ ἵκηται, κενεὰ πνεύσαις ἔπορε μόχθῳ
 βραχύ τι τερπνόν. τὶν δ' ἀδυεπής τε λύρα
γλυκύς τ' αὐλὸς ἀναπάσσει χάριν·
95 τρέφοντι δ' εὐρὺ κλέος
κόραι Πιερίδες Διός.

22

and all the sanctuary rang with singing amid festive joy   Ep. 4
in the fashion of victory celebration.
And faithful to those ancient beginnings,
    now too we shall sing a song of glory named
for proud victory to celebrate the thunder
and fire-flung weapon   80
of thunder-rousing Zeus,
the blazing lightning
that befits every triumph,
and the swelling strains of song
    shall answer to the pipe's reed,

songs that have at last appeared by famous Dirke.[4]   Str. 5
But as a son, born from his wife, is longed for   86
by a father already come to the opposite of youth
    and warms his mind with great love
(since wealth that falls to the care
of a stranger from elsewhere
is most hateful to a dying man),   90

so, when a man who has performed noble deeds,   Ant. 5
Hagesidamos, goes without song to Hades'
dwelling, in vain has he striven and gained for his toil
    but brief delight. Upon you, however, the sweetly
speaking lyre and melodious pipe are shedding glory,
and the Pierian daughters of Zeus[5]   95
are fostering your widespread fame.

[4] The spring near Pindar's Thebes.
[5] The Muses were born in Pieria, north of Mt. Olympos (cf. Hes. *Th.* 53).

ἐγὼ δὲ συνεφαπτόμενος σπουδᾷ, κλυτὸν ἔθνος
Λοκρῶν ἀμφέπεσον, μέλιτι
εὐάνορα πόλιν καταβρέχων·
    παῖδ᾽ ἐρατὸν ⟨δ᾽⟩ Ἀρχεστράτου
100 αἴνησα, τὸν εἶδον κρατέοντα χερὸς ἀλκᾷ
βωμὸν παρ᾽ Ὀλύμπιον
κεῖνον κατὰ χρόνον
ἰδέᾳ τε καλόν
ὥρᾳ τε κεκραμένον, ἅ ποτε
105 ἀναιδέα Γανυμήδει μόρον ἄ-
    λαλκε σὺν Κυπρογενεῖ.

And I have earnestly joined in and embraced   Ep. 5
the famous race of the Lokrians, drenching with honey
their city of brave men.
    I have praised the lovely son of Archestratos,
whom I saw winning with the strength of his hand   100
by the Olympic altar
at that time,
beautiful of form
and imbued with the youthfulness that once averted
ruthless death from Ganymede,   105
    with the aid of the Cyprus-born goddess.[6]

[6] Aphrodite.

SOPHOCLES

Translation by Hugh Lloyd-Jones

ΦΥΛΑΞ

ταύτην γ᾽ ἰδὼν θάπτουσαν ὃν σὺ τὸν νεκρὸν
405 ἀπεῖπας. ἆρ᾽ ἔνδηλα καὶ σαφῆ λέγω;

ΚΡΕΩΝ

καὶ πῶς ὁρᾶται κἀπίληπτος ᾑρέθη;

ΦΥΛΑΞ

τοιοῦτον ἦν τὸ πρᾶγμ᾽. ὅπως γὰρ ἥκομεν,
πρὸς σοῦ τὰ δείν᾽ ἐκεῖν᾽ ἐπηπειλημένοι,
πᾶσαν κόνιν σήραντες ἣ κατεῖχε τὸν
410 νέκυν, μυδῶν τε σῶμα γυμνώσαντες εὖ,
καθήμεθ᾽ ἄκρων ἐκ πάγων ὑπήνεμοι,
ὀσμὴν ἀπ᾽ αὐτοῦ μὴ βάλῃ πεφευγότες,
ἐγερτὶ κινῶν ἄνδρ᾽ ἀνὴρ ἐπιρρόθοις
κακοῖσιν, εἴ τις τοῦδ᾽ ἀφειδήσοι πόνου.
415 χρόνον τάδ᾽ ἦν τοσοῦτον, ἔστ᾽ ἐν αἰθέρι
μέσῳ κατέστη λαμπρὸς ἡλίου κύκλος
καὶ καῦμ᾽ ἔθαλπε· καὶ τότ᾽ ἐξαίφνης χθονὸς

26

Antigone 404–485

One woman's conscience against the state: Antigone,
defying the king, gives her punished brother
a decent burial

GUARD

Yes, I saw her burying the corpse whose burial you for-
bade! Is what I say clear and exact?

CREON

And how was she sighted and taken in the act?

GUARD

It was like this! When we went back, after those terrible
threats of yours, we swept away all the dust that covered
the corpse, carefully stripped the mouldering body, and
then sat shielded by the hilltops from the wind, avoiding
the smell that might have come to us from it, each man
watchfully arousing his neighbour with volleys of abuse, if
anyone seemed likely to neglect this task. This lasted until
the bright circle of the sun took its place in the sky and the
midday heat began to roast us; and then suddenly a whirl-

SOPHOCLES

τυφὼς ἀγείρας σκηπτόν, οὐράνιον ἄχος,
πίμπλησι πεδίον, πᾶσαν αἰκίζων φόβην
420 ὕλης πεδιάδος, ἐν δ' ἐμεστώθη μέγας
αἰθήρ· μύσαντες δ' εἴχομεν θείαν νόσον.
καὶ τοῦδ' ἀπαλλαγέντος ἐν χρόνῳ μακρῷ,
ἡ παῖς ὁρᾶται κἀνακωκύει πικρῶς
ὄρνιθος ὀξὺν φθόγγον, ὡς ὅταν κενῆς
425 εὐνῆς νεοσσῶν ὀρφανὸν βλέψῃ λέχος·
οὕτω δὲ χαὔτη, ψιλὸν ὡς ὁρᾷ νέκυν,
γόοισιν ἐξῴμωξεν, ἐκ δ' ἀρὰς κακὰς
ἠρᾶτο τοῖσι τοὔργον ἐξειργασμένοις.
καὶ χερσὶν εὐθὺς διψίαν φέρει κόνιν,
430 ἔκ τ' εὐκροτήτου χαλκέας ἄρδην πρόχου
χοαῖσι τρισπόνδοισι τὸν νέκυν στέφει.
χἠμεῖς ἰδόντες ἱέμεσθα, σὺν δέ νιν
θηρώμεθ' εὐθὺς οὐδὲν ἐκπεπληγμένην,
καὶ τάς τε πρόσθεν τάς τε νῦν ἠλέγχομεν
435 πράξεις· ἄπαρνος δ' οὐδενὸς καθίστατο,
ἅμ' ἡδέως ἔμοιγε κἀλγεινῶς ἅμα.
τὸ μὲν γὰρ αὐτὸν ἐκ κακῶν πεφευγέναι
ἥδιστον, ἐς κακὸν δὲ τοὺς φίλους ἄγειν
ἀλγεινόν. ἀλλὰ πάντα ταῦθ' ἥσσω λαβεῖν
440 ἐμοὶ πέφυκε τῆς ἐμῆς σωτηρίας.

ΚΡΕΩΝ
σὲ δή, σὲ τὴν νεύουσαν ἐς πέδον κάρα,
φής, ἢ καταρνῇ μὴ δεδρακέναι τάδε;

28

wind on the ground raised up a storm, a trouble in the air, and filled the plain, tormenting all the foliage of the woods that covered the ground there; and the vast sky was filled with it, and we shut our eyes and endured the godsent affliction.

And when after a long time this went away, we saw the girl; she cried out bitterly, with a sound like the piercing note of a bird when she sees her empty nest robbed of her young; just so did she cry out, weeping, when she saw the corpse laid bare and called down curses on those who had done the deed. At once she brought in her hands thirsty dust, and from the well-wrought brazen urn that she was carrying she poured over the corpse a threefold libation. When we saw it we made haste and at once seized her, she being in no way surprised, and charged her with her earlier action and with this. She denied none of it, which gave me pleasure and pain at once. For to have escaped oneself from trouble is most pleasant, but to bring friends into danger is painful. But all this matters less to me than my own safety!

CREON

You there, you that are bowing down your head towards the ground, do you admit, or do you deny, that you have done this?

SOPHOCLES

ΑΝΤΙΓΟΝΗ

καὶ φημὶ δρᾶσαι κοὐκ ἀπαρνοῦμαι τὸ μή.

ΚΡΕΩΝ

σὺ μὲν κομίζοις ἂν σεαυτὸν ᾗ θέλεις
445 ἔξω βαρείας αἰτίας ἐλεύθερον·
σὺ δ' εἰπέ μοι μὴ μῆκος, ἀλλὰ συντόμως,
ᾔδησθα κηρυχθέντα μὴ πράσσειν τάδε;

ΑΝΤΙΓΟΝΗ

ᾔδη· τί δ' οὐκ ἔμελλον; ἐμφανῆ γὰρ ἦν.

ΚΡΕΩΝ

καὶ δῆτ' ἐτόλμας τούσδ' ὑπερβαίνειν νόμους;

ΑΝΤΙΓΟΝΗ

450 οὐ γάρ τί μοι Ζεὺς ἦν ὁ κηρύξας τάδε,
οὐδ' ἡ ξύνοικος τῶν κάτω θεῶν Δίκη
τοιούσδ' ἐν ἀνθρώποισιν ὥρισεν νόμους·
οὐδὲ σθένειν τοσοῦτον ᾠόμην τὰ σὰ
κηρύγμαθ' ὥστ' ἄγραπτα κἀσφαλῆ θεῶν
455 νόμιμα δύνασθαι θνητά γ' ὄνθ' ὑπερδραμεῖν.
οὐ γάρ τι νῦν γε κἀχθές, ἀλλ' ἀεί ποτε
ζῇ ταῦτα, κοὐδεὶς οἶδεν ἐξ ὅτου 'φάνη.
τούτων ἐγὼ οὐκ ἔμελλον, ἀνδρὸς οὐδενὸς
φρόνημα δείσασ', ἐν θεοῖσι τὴν δίκην
460 δώσειν· θανουμένη γὰρ ἐξῄδη, τί δ' οὔ;
κεἰ μὴ σὺ προὐκήρυξας. εἰ δὲ τοῦ χρόνου
πρόσθεν θανοῦμαι, κέρδος αὔτ' ἐγὼ λέγω.
ὅστις γὰρ ἐν πολλοῖσιν ὡς ἐγὼ κακοῖς
ζῇ, πῶς ὅδ' οὐχὶ κατθανὼν κέρδος φέρει;

ANTIGONE

ANTIGONE
I say that I did it and I do not deny it.

CREON
(*to GUARD*) You may take yourself to wherever you please, free from the heavy charge.

Exit GUARD.

(*to ANTIGONE*) But do you tell me, not at length, but briefly: did you know of the proclamation forbidding this?

ANTIGONE
I knew it; of course I knew it. It was known to all.

CREON
And yet you dared to transgress these laws?

ANTIGONE
Yes, for it was not Zeus who made this proclamation, nor was it Justice who lives with the gods below that established such laws among men, nor did I think your proclamations strong enough to have power to overrule, mortal as they were, the unwritten and unfailing ordinances of the gods. For these have life, not simply today and yesterday, but for ever, and no one knows how long ago they were revealed. For this I did not intend to pay the penalty among the gods for fear of any man's pride. I knew that I would die, of course I knew, even if you had made no proclamation. But if I die before my time, I account that gain. For does not whoever lives among many troubles, as I do, gain

465 οὕτως ἔμοιγε τοῦδε τοῦ μόρου τυχεῖν
παρ' οὐδὲν ἄλγος· ἀλλ' ἄν, εἰ τὸν ἐξ ἐμῆς
μητρὸς θανόντ' ἄθαπτον ⟨ὄντ'⟩ ἠνεσχόμην,
κείνοις ἂν ἤλγουν· τοῖσδε δ' οὐκ ἀλγύνομαι.
σοὶ δ' εἰ δοκῶ νῦν μῶρα δρῶσα τυγχάνειν,
470 σχεδόν τι μώρῳ μωρίαν ὀφλισκάνω.

ΧΟΡΟΣ
δῆλον· τὸ γέννημ' ὠμὸν ἐξ ὠμοῦ πατρὸς
τῆς παιδός· εἴκειν δ' οὐκ ἐπίσταται κακοῖς.

ΚΡΕΩΝ
ἀλλ' ἴσθι τοι τὰ σκλήρ' ἄγαν φρονήματα
πίπτειν μάλιστα, καὶ τὸν ἐγκρατέστατον
475 σίδηρον ὀπτὸν ἐκ πυρὸς περισκελῆ
θραυσθέντα καὶ ῥαγέντα πλεῖστ' ἂν εἰσίδοις.
σμικρῷ χαλινῷ δ' οἶδα τοὺς θυμουμένους
ἵππους καταρτυθέντας· οὐ γὰρ ἐκπέλει
φρονεῖν μέγ' ὅστις δοῦλός ἐστι τῶν πέλας.
480 αὕτη δ' ὑβρίζειν μὲν τότ' ἐξηπίστατο,
νόμους ὑπερβαίνουσα τοὺς προκειμένους·
ὕβρις δ', ἐπεὶ δέδρακεν, ἥδε δευτέρα,
τούτοις ἐπαυχεῖν καὶ δεδρακυῖαν γελᾶν.
ἦ νῦν ἐγὼ μὲν οὐκ ἀνήρ, αὕτη δ' ἀνήρ,
485 εἰ ταῦτ' ἀνατεὶ τῇδε κείσεται κράτη.

by death? So it is in no way painful for me to meet with this death; if I had endured that the son of my own mother should die and remain unburied, that would have given me pain, but this gives me none. And if you think my actions foolish, that amounts to a charge of folly by a fool!

CHORUS

It is clear! The nature of the girl is savage, like her father's, and she does not know how to bend before her troubles.

CREON

Why, know that over-stubborn wills are the most apt to fall, and the toughest iron, baked in the fire till it is hard, is most often, you will see, cracked and shattered! I know that spirited horses are controlled by a small bridle; for pride is impossible for anyone who is another's slave. This girl knew well how to be insolent then, transgressing the established laws; and after her action, this was a second insolence, to exult in this and to laugh at the thought of having done it. Indeed, now I am no man, but she is a man, if she is to enjoy such power as this with impunity.

EURIPIDES

Translation by David Kovacs

ΜΗΔΕΙΑ

ὦ Ζεῦ Δίκη τε Ζηνὸς Ἡλίου τε φῶς,
765 νῦν καλλίνικοι τῶν ἐμῶν ἐχθρῶν, φίλαι,
γενησόμεσθα κεἰς ὁδὸν βεβήκαμεν,
νῦν ἐλπὶς ἐχθροὺς τοὺς ἐμοὺς τείσειν δίκην.
οὗτος γὰρ ἁνὴρ ᾗ μάλιστ᾽ ἐκάμνομεν
λιμὴν πέφανται τῶν ἐμῶν βουλευμάτων·
770 ἐκ τοῦδ᾽ ἀναψόμεσθα πρυμνήτην κάλων,
μολόντες ἄστυ καὶ πόλισμα Παλλάδος.
  ἤδη δὲ πάντα τἀμά σοι βουλεύματα
λέξω· δέχου δὲ μὴ πρὸς ἡδονὴν λόγους.
πέμψασ᾽ ἐμῶν τιν᾽ οἰκετῶν Ἰάσονα
775 ἐς ὄψιν ἐλθεῖν τὴν ἐμὴν αἰτήσομαι.
μολόντι δ᾽ αὐτῷ μαλθακοὺς λέξω λόγους,
ὡς καὶ δοκεῖ μοι ταὐτὰ καὶ καλῶς γαμεῖ

Medea 764–865

Medea, offered asylum at Athens, proceeds to plot
her revenge against Jason, who has left her
for another woman

MEDEA

O Zeus and Zeus's justice, O light of the sun, now, my
friends, I shall be victorious over my foes: I have set my
foot on the path. Now I may confidently expect that my en-
emies will pay the penalty. For this man,[1] at the very point
where I was most in trouble, has appeared as a harbor for
my plans: to him will I tie my stern cable when I go to the
city of Pallas Athena.

Now I shall reveal to you my entire design. Hear, then,
words that will give you no pleasure. I shall send one of my
servants and ask Jason to come to see me. When he arrives,
I shall speak soothing words to him, saying that I hold the
same opinion as he, that the royal marriage he has made by

---

[1] Aegeus, king of Athens.

γάμους τυράννων οὓς προδοὺς ἡμᾶς ἔχει,
καὶ ξύμφορ᾽ εἶναι καὶ καλῶς ἐγνωσμένα.
780 παῖδας δὲ μεῖναι τοὺς ἐμοὺς αἰτήσομαι,
οὐχ ὡς λιποῦσ᾽ ἂν πολεμίας ἐπὶ χθονὸς
ἐχθροῖσι παῖδας τοὺς ἐμοὺς καθυβρίσαι,
ἀλλ᾽ ὡς δόλοισι παῖδα βασιλέως κτάνω.
πέμψω γὰρ αὐτοὺς δῶρ᾽ ἔχοντας ἐν χεροῖν,
785 [νύμφῃ φέροντας, τήνδε μὴ φεύγειν χθόνα,]
λεπτόν τε πέπλον καὶ πλόκον χρυσήλατον·
κἄνπερ λαβοῦσα κόσμον ἀμφιθῇ χροΐ,
κακῶς ὀλεῖται πᾶς θ᾽ ὃς ἂν θίγῃ κόρης·
τοιοῖσδε χρίσω φαρμάκοις δωρήματα.
790   ἐνταῦθα μέντοι τόνδ᾽ ἀπαλλάσσω λόγον.
ᾤμωξα δ᾽ οἷον ἔργον ἔστ᾽ ἐργαστέον
τοὐντεῦθεν ἡμῖν· τέκνα γὰρ κατακτενῶ
τἄμ᾽· οὔτις ἔστιν ὅστις ἐξαιρήσεται·
δόμον τε πάντα συγχέασ᾽ Ἰάσονος
795 ἔξειμι γαίας, φιλτάτων παίδων φόνον
φεύγουσα καὶ τλᾶσ᾽ ἔργον ἀνοσιώτατον.
οὐ γὰρ γελᾶσθαι τλητὸν ἐξ ἐχθρῶν, φίλαι.
ἴτω· τί μοι ζῆν κέρδος; οὔτε μοι πατρὶς
οὔτ᾽ οἶκος ἔστιν οὔτ᾽ ἀποστροφὴ κακῶν.
800 ἡμάρτανον τόθ᾽ ἡνίκ᾽ ἐξελίμπανον
δόμους πατρῴους, ἀνδρὸς Ἕλληνος λόγοις
πεισθεῖσ᾽, ὃς ἡμῖν σὺν θεῷ τείσει δίκην.
οὔτ᾽ ἐξ ἐμοῦ γὰρ παῖδας ὄψεταί ποτε
ζῶντας τὸ λοιπὸν οὔτε τῆς νεοζύγου
805 νύμφης τεκνώσει παῖδ᾽, ἐπεὶ κακὴν κακῶς

abandoning me is well made, that these are beneficial and good decisions. I shall ask that the children be allowed to stay, not with the thought that I might leave them behind on hostile soil for my enemies to insult, but so that I may kill the princess by guile. I shall send them bearing gifts, [bearing them to the bride so as not to be exiled,] a finely woven gown and a diadem of beaten gold. If she takes this finery and puts it on, she will die a painful death, and likewise anyone who touches her: with such poisons will I smear these gifts.

This subject, however, I now leave behind. Ah me, I groan at what a deed I must do next! I shall kill my children: there is no one who can rescue them. When I have utterly confounded the whole house of Jason, I shall leave the land, in flight from the murder of my own dear sons, having committed a most unholy deed. The laughter of one's enemies is unendurable, my friends. Let that be as it will. What do I gain by living? I have no fatherland, no house, and no means to turn aside misfortune. My mistake was when I left my father's house, persuaded by the words of a Greek. This man—a god being my helper—will pay for what he has done to me. He shall never from this day see

θανεῖν σφ᾽ ἀνάγκη τοῖς ἐμοῖσι φαρμάκοις.
μηδείς με φαύλην κἀσθενῆ νομιζέτω
μηδ᾽ ἡσυχαίαν, ἀλλὰ θατέρου τρόπου,
βαρεῖαν ἐχθροῖς καὶ φίλοισιν εὐμενῆ·
810 τῶν γὰρ τοιούτων εὐκλεέστατος βίος.

ΧΟΡΟΣ

ἐπείπερ ἡμῖν τόνδ᾽ ἐκοίνωσας λόγον,
σέ τ᾽ ὠφελεῖν θέλουσα καὶ νόμοις βροτῶν
ξυλλαμβάνουσα δρᾶν σ᾽ ἀπεννέπω τάδε.

ΜΗΔΕΙΑ

οὐκ ἔστιν ἄλλως· σοὶ δὲ συγγνώμη λέγειν
815 τάδ᾽ ἐστί, μὴ πάσχουσαν, ὡς ἐγώ, κακῶς.

ΧΟΡΟΣ

ἀλλὰ κτανεῖν σὸν σπέρμα τολμήσεις, γύναι;

ΜΗΔΕΙΑ

οὕτω γὰρ ἂν μάλιστα δηχθείη πόσις.

ΧΟΡΟΣ

σὺ δ᾽ ἂν γένοιό γ᾽ ἀθλιωτάτη γυνή.

ΜΗΔΕΙΑ

ἴτω· περισσοὶ πάντες οὑν μέσῳ λόγοι.
820   ἀλλ᾽ εἶα χώρει καὶ κόμιζ᾽ Ἰάσονα
(ἐς πάντα γὰρ δὴ σοὶ τὰ πιστὰ χρώμεθα)
λέξῃς δὲ μηδὲν τῶν ἐμοὶ δεδογμένων,
εἴπερ φρονεῖς εὖ δεσπόταις γυνή τ᾽ ἔφυς.

his children by me alive, nor will he have children by his
new bride since that wretch must die a wretched death by
my poisons. Let no one think me weak, contemptible, un-
troublesome. No, quite the opposite, hurtful to foes, to
friends kindly. Such persons live a life of greatest glory.

CHORUS LEADER

Since you have shared this plan with me, and since I wish
to help you and uphold the laws of society, I urge you not to
do this deed.

MEDEA

It cannot be otherwise. I excuse you for speaking thus
since you have not suffered as I have.

CHORUS LEADER

Yet will you bring yourself to kill your own offspring,
woman?

MEDEA

It is the way to hurt my husband most.

CHORUS LEADER

And for yourself to become the most wretched of women.

MEDEA

Be that as it may. Till then all talk is superfluous.

(to the Nurse) But you, go and fetch Jason (for I use
your service on all errands of trust). Tell him nothing of my
intentions, if you are loyal to your mistress and a woman.

Exit Nurse by Eisodos B, MEDEA into the house.

EURIPIDES

στρ. α

Ἐρεχθεῖδαι τὸ παλαιὸν ὄλβιοι
825   καὶ θεῶν παῖδες μακάρων, ἱερᾶς
χώρας ἀπορθήτου τ᾽ ἄπο, φερβόμενοι
κλεινοτάταν σοφίαν, αἰεὶ διὰ λαμπροτάτου
830   βαίνοντες ἀβρῶς αἰθέρος, ἔνθα ποθ᾽ ἁγνὰς
ἐννέα Πιερίδας Μούσας λέγουσι
ξανθὰν Ἁρμονίαν φυτεῦσαι·

ἀντ. α

835   τοῦ καλλινάου τ᾽ ἐπὶ Κηφισοῦ ῥοαῖς
τὰν Κύπριν κλῄζουσιν ἀφυσσαμέναν
χώρας καταπνεῦσαι μετρίους ἀνέμων
840   ἀέρας ἡδυπνόους· αἰεὶ δ᾽ ἐπιβαλλομέναν
χαίταισιν εὐώδη ῥοδέων πλόκον ἀνθέων
τᾷ Σοφίᾳ παρέδρους πέμπειν Ἔρωτας,
845   παντοίας ἀρετᾶς ξυνεργούς.

στρ. β

πῶς οὖν ἱερῶν ποταμῶν
ἢ πόλις ἢ θεῶν
πόμπιμός σε χώρα
τὰν παιδολέτειραν ἕξει,
850   τὰν οὐχ ὁσίαν, μετ᾽ ἀστῶν;
σκέψαι τεκέων πλαγάν,
σκέψαι φόνον οἷον αἴρῃ.
μή, πρὸς γονάτων σε πάν-
τα πάντως ἱκετεύομεν,
855   τέκνα φονεύσῃς.

40

CHORUS

From ancient times the sons of Erechtheus have been favored; they are children of the blessed gods sprung from a holy land never pillaged by the enemy. They feed on wisdom most glorious, always stepping gracefully through the bright air, where once, it is said, the nine Pierian Muses gave birth to fair-haired Harmonia.

Men celebrate in song how Aphrodite, filling her pail at the streams of the fair-flowing Cephisus, blew down upon the land temperate and sweet breezes. And ever dressing her hair with a fragrant chaplet of roses she sends the Loves to sit at Wisdom's side, joint workers in every kind of excellence.

How then shall this city of holy rivers or this land that escorts its gods in procession lodge you, the killer of your children, stained with their blood, in the company of her citizens? Think on the slaying of your children, think what slaughter you are committing! Do not, we beseech you by your knees and in every way we can, do not kill your children!

ἀντ. β

πόθεν θράσος ἢ φρενὸς ἢ
χειρὶ †τέκνων† σέθεν
καρδίᾳ τε λήψῃ
δεινὰν προσάγουσα τόλμαν;
860   πῶς δ' ὄμματα προσβαλοῦσα
τέκνοις ἄδακρυν μοῖραν
σχήσεις φόνου; οὐ δυνάσῃ,
παίδων ἱκετᾶν πιτνόν-
των, τέγξαι χέρα φοινίαν
865   τλάμονι θυμῷ.

MEDEA

How will you summon up the strength of purpose or the courage of hand and heart to dare this dreadful deed? When you have turned your eyes upon your children, how will you behold their fate with tearless eye? When your children fall as suppliants at your feet, you will not be hard-hearted enough to drench your hand in their blood.

HERODOTUS

Translation by A. D. Godley

1. Ἡροδότου Ἁλικαρνησσέος ἱστορίης ἀπόδεξις
ἥδε, ὡς μήτε τὰ γενόμενα ἐξ ἀνθρώπων τῷ χρόνῳ
ἐξίτηλα γένηται, μήτε ἔργα μεγάλα τε καὶ θωμαστά,
τὰ μὲν Ἕλλησι τὰ δὲ βαρβάροισι ἀποδεχθέντα,
ἀκλεᾶ γένηται, τά τε ἄλλα καὶ δι᾽ ἣν αἰτίην
ἐπολέμησαν ἀλλήλοισι.

Περσέων μέν νυν οἱ λόγιοι Φοίνικας αἰτίους φασὶ
γενέσθαι τῆς διαφορῆς. τούτους γὰρ ἀπὸ τῆς
Ἐρυθρῆς καλεομένης θαλάσσης ἀπικομένους ἐπὶ
τήνδε τὴν θάλασσαν, καὶ οἰκήσαντας τοῦτον τὸν
χῶρον τὸν καὶ νῦν οἰκέουσι, αὐτίκα ναυτιλίῃσι
μακρῇσι ἐπιθέσθαι, ἀπαγινέοντας δὲ φορτία
Αἰγύπτιά τε καὶ Ἀσσύρια τῇ τε ἄλλη ἐσαπικνέεσθαι
καὶ δὴ καὶ ἐς Ἄργος. τὸ δὲ Ἄργος τοῦτον τὸν χρόνον
προεῖχε ἅπασι τῶν ἐν τῇ νῦν Ἑλλάδι καλεομένη
χώρῃ. ἀπικομένους δὲ τοὺς Φοίνικας ἐς δὴ τὸ Ἄργος
τοῦτο διατίθεσθαι τὸν φόρτον. πέμπτῃ δὲ ἢ ἕκτῃ
ἡμέρῃ ἀπ᾽ ἧς ἀπίκοντο, ἐξεμπολημένων σφι σχεδὸν

Persian Wars 1.1–4

An account of the causes of the conflict between
the Greeks and the Persians

1. What Herodotus the Halicarnassian has learnt by
inquiry is here set forth: in order that so the memory of the
past may not be blotted out from among men by time, and
that great and marvellous deeds done by Greeks and for-
eigners and especially the reason why they warred against
each other may not lack renown.

The Persian learned men say that the Phoenicians were
the cause of the feud. These (they say) came to our seas
from the sea which is called Red,[1] and having settled in the
country which they still occupy, at once began to make
long voyages. Among other places to which they carried
Egyptian and Assyrian merchandise, they came to Argos,
which was about that time preeminent in every way among
the people of what is now called Hellas. The Phoenicians
then came, as I say, to Argos, and set out their cargo. On
the fifth or sixth day from their coming, their wares being

[1] Not the modern Red Sea, but the Persian Gulf and adjacent
waters.

πάντων, ἐλθεῖν ἐπὶ τὴν θάλασσαν γυναῖκας ἄλλας τε
πολλὰς καὶ δὴ καὶ τοῦ βασιλέος θυγατέρα· τὸ δέ οἱ
οὔνομα εἶναι, κατὰ τὠυτὸ τὸ καὶ Ἕλληνες λέγουσι,
Ἰοῦν τὴν Ἰνάχου· ταύτας στάσας κατὰ πρύμνην τῆς
νεὸς ὠνέεσθαι τῶν φορτίων τῶν σφι ἦν θυμὸς
μάλιστα· καὶ τοὺς Φοίνικας διακελευσαμένους
ὁρμῆσαι ἐπ' αὐτάς. τὰς μὲν δὴ πλεῦνας τῶν γυναικῶν
ἀποφυγεῖν, τὴν δὲ Ἰοῦν σὺν ἄλλῃσι ἁρπασθῆναι.
ἐσβαλομένους δὲ ἐς τὴν νέα οἴχεσθαι ἀποπλέοντας
ἐπ' Αἰγύπτου.

2. Οὕτω μὲν Ἰοῦν ἐς Αἴγυπτον ἀπικέσθαι λέγουσι
Πέρσαι, οὐκ ὡς Ἕλληνες, καὶ τῶν ἀδικημάτων
πρῶτον τοῦτο ἄρξαι. μετὰ δὲ ταῦτα Ἑλλήνων τινάς
(οὐ γὰρ ἔχουσι τοὔνομα ἀπηγήσασθαι) φασὶ τῆς
Φοινίκης ἐς Τύρον προσσχόντας ἁρπάσαι τοῦ
βασιλέος τὴν θυγατέρα Εὐρώπην. εἴησαν δ' ἂν οὗτοι
Κρῆτες. ταῦτα μὲν δὴ ἴσα πρὸς ἴσα σφι γενέσθαι,
μετὰ δὲ ταῦτα Ἕλληνας αἰτίους τῆς δευτέρης ἀδικίης
γενέσθαι· καταπλώσαντας γὰρ μακρῇ νηῒ ἐς Αἶάν τε
τὴν Κολχίδα καὶ ἐπὶ Φᾶσιν ποταμόν, ἐνθεῦτεν,
διαπρηξαμένους καὶ τἆλλα τῶν εἵνεκεν ἀπίκατο,
ἁρπάσαι τοῦ βασιλέος τὴν θυγατέρα Μηδείην.
πέμψαντα δὲ τὸν Κόλχων βασιλέα ἐς τὴν Ἑλλάδα
κήρυκα αἰτέειν τε δίκας τῆς ἁρπαγῆς καὶ ἀπαιτέειν
τὴν θυγατέρα. τοὺς δὲ ὑποκρίνασθαι ὡς οὐδὲ ἐκεῖνοι
Ἰοῦς τῆς Ἀργείης ἔδοσάν σφι δίκας τῆς ἁρπαγῆς·
οὐδὲ ὧν αὐτοὶ δώσειν ἐκείνοισι.

3. Δευτέρῃ δὲ λέγουσι γενεῇ μετὰ ταῦτα

now well-nigh all sold, there came to the sea shore among many other women the king's daughter, whose name (according to Persians and Greeks alike) was Io, the daughter of Inachus. They stood about the stern of the ship: and while they bargained for such wares as they fancied, the Phoenicians heartened each other to the deed, and rushed to take them. Most of the women escaped: Io with others was carried off; the men cast her into the ship and made sail away for Egypt.

2. This, say the Persians (but not the Greeks), was how Io came to Egypt, and this, according to them, was the first wrong that was done. Next, according to their tale, certain Greeks (they cannot tell who) landed at Tyre in Phoenice and carried off the king's daughter Europe. These Greeks must, I suppose, have been Cretans. So far, then, the account between them stood balanced. But after this (say they) it was the Greeks who were guilty of the second wrong. They sailed in a long ship to Aea of the Colchians and the river Phasis:[2] and when they had done the rest of the business for which they came, they carried off the king's daughter Medea. When the Colchian king sent a herald to demand reparation for the robbery, and restitution of his daughter, the Greeks replied that as they had been refused reparation for the abduction of the Argive Io, neither would they make any to the Colchians.

3. Then (so the story runs) in the second generation af-

[2] This is the legendary cruise of the Argonauts.

Ἀλέξανδρον τὸν Πριάμου, ἀκηκοότα ταῦτα, ἐθελῆσαί
οἱ ἐκ τῆς Ἑλλάδος δι᾽ ἁρπαγῆς γενέσθαι γυναῖκα,
ἐπιστάμενον πάντως ὅτι οὐ δώσει δίκας· οὐδὲ γὰρ
ἐκείνους διδόναι. οὕτω δὴ ἁρπάσαντος αὐτοῦ Ἑλένην,
τοῖσι Ἕλλησι δόξαι πρῶτον πέμψαντας ἀγγέλους
ἀπαιτέειν τε Ἑλένην καὶ δίκας τῆς ἁρπαγῆς αἰτέειν.
τοὺς δέ, προϊσχομένων ταῦτα, προφέρειν σφι
Μηδείης τὴν ἁρπαγήν, ὡς οὐ δόντες αὐτοὶ δίκας οὐδὲ
ἐκδόντες ἀπαιτεόντων βουλοίατό σφι παρ᾽ ἄλλων
δίκας γίνεσθαι.

4. Μέχρι μὲν ὦν τούτου ἁρπαγὰς μούνας εἶναι
παρ᾽ ἀλλήλων, τὸ δὲ ἀπὸ τούτου Ἕλληνας δὴ
μεγάλως αἰτίους γενέσθαι· προτέρους γὰρ ἄρξαι
στρατεύεσθαι ἐς τὴν Ἀσίην ἢ σφέας ἐς τὴν Εὐρώπην.
τὸ μέν νυν ἁρπάζειν γυναῖκας ἀνδρῶν ἀδίκων νομίζειν
ἔργον εἶναι, τὸ δὲ ἁρπασθεισέων σπουδὴν
ποιήσασθαι τιμωρέειν ἀνοήτων, τὸ δὲ μηδεμίαν ὤρην
ἔχειν ἁρπασθεισέων σωφρόνων· δῆλα γὰρ δὴ ὅτι, εἰ
μὴ αὐταὶ ἐβούλοντο, οὐκ ἂν ἡρπάζοντο. σφέας μὲν δὴ
τοὺς ἐκ τῆς Ἀσίης λέγουσι Πέρσαι ἁρπαζομενέων
τῶν γυναικῶν λόγον οὐδένα ποιήσασθαι, Ἕλληνας δὲ
Λακεδαιμονίης εἵνεκεν γυναικὸς στόλον μέγαν
συναγεῖραι καὶ ἔπειτα ἐλθόντας ἐς τὴν Ἀσίην τὴν
Πριάμου δύναμιν κατελεῖν. ἀπὸ τούτου αἰεὶ
ἡγήσασθαι τὸ Ἑλληνικὸν σφίσι εἶναι πολέμιον. τὴν
γὰρ Ἀσίην καὶ τὰ ἐνοικέοντα ἔθνεα βάρβαρα
οἰκιεῦνται οἱ Πέρσαι, τὴν δὲ Εὐρώπην καὶ τὸ
Ἑλληνικὸν ἥγηνται κεχωρίσθαι.

ter this Alexandrus[3] son of Priam, having heard this tale, was minded to win himself a wife out of Hellas by ravishment; for he was well persuaded that, as the Greeks had made no reparation, so neither would he. So he carried off Helen. The Greeks first resolved to send messengers demanding that Helen should be restored and atonement made for the rape; but when this proposal was made, the Trojans pleaded the rape of Medea, and reminded the Greeks that they asked reparation of others, yet had made none themselves, nor given up the plunder at request.

4. Thus far it was a matter of mere robbery on both sides. But after this (the Persians say) the Greeks were greatly to blame; for they invaded Asia before the Persians attacked Europe. "We think," say they, "that it is wrong to carry women off: but to be zealous to avenge the rape is foolish: wise men take no account of such things: for plainly the women would never have been carried away, had not they themselves wished it. We of Asia regarded the rape of our women not at all; but the Greeks, all for the sake of a Lacedaemonian woman, mustered a great host, came to Asia, and destroyed the power of Priam. Ever since then we have regarded Greeks as our enemies." The Persians claim Asia for their own, and the foreign nations that dwell in it; Europe and the Greek race they hold to be separate from them.

[3] I.e., Paris.

THUCYDIDES

Translation by Charles Forster Smith

Καὶ ὁ Νικίας γνοὺς ὅτι ἀπὸ μὲν τῶν αὐτῶν λόγων οὐκ
ἂν ἔτι ἀποτρέψειε, παρασκευῆς δὲ πλήθει, εἰ πολλὴν
ἐπιτάξειε, τάχ᾽ ἂν μεταστήσειεν αὐτούς, παρελθὼν
αὐτοῖς αὖθις ἔλεγε τοίαδε.

XX. "Ἐπειδὴ πάντως ὁρῶ ὑμᾶς, ὦ Ἀθηναῖοι,
ὡρμημένους στρατεύειν, ξυνενέγκοι μὲν ταῦτα ὡς
βουλόμεθα, ἐπὶ δὲ τῷ παρόντι ἃ γιγνώσκω σημανῶ.
2 ἐπὶ γὰρ πόλεις, ὡς ἐγὼ ἀκοῇ αἰσθάνομαι, μέλλομεν
ἰέναι μεγάλας καὶ οὔθ᾽ ὑπηκόους ἀλλήλων οὐδὲ
δεομένας μεταβολῆς, ᾗ ἂν ἐκ βιαίου τις δουλείας ἄσ-
μενος ἐς ῥᾴω μετάστασιν χωροίη, οὔτ᾽ ἂν τὴν ἀρχὴν
τὴν ἡμετέραν εἰκότως ἀντ᾽ ἐλευθερίας προσδεξαμένας,
τό τε πλῆθος, ὡς ἐν μιᾷ νήσῳ, πολλὰς Ἑλληνίδας.
3 πλὴν γὰρ Νάξου καὶ Κατάνης, ἃς ἐλπίζω ἡμῖν κατὰ
τὸ Λεοντίνων ξυγγενὲς προσέσεσθαι, ἄλλαι εἰσὶν

History of the Peloponnesian War 6.19.2–24.4

The Athenian general Nicias attempts to dissuade
his countrymen from invading Sicily

And Nicias, seeing that he could no longer deter them
with the same arguments, but thinking that by the mag-
nitude of the armament, if he insisted upon a large one,
he might possibly change their minds, came forward and
spoke as follows:

XX. "Since I see, men of Athens, that you are wholly
bent upon the expedition, I pray that these matters may
turn out as we wish; for the present juncture, however, I
will show what my judgment is. The cities we are about to
attack are, as I learn by report, large, and neither subject to
one another nor in need of any such change as a person
might be happy to accept in order to escape from enforced
servitude to an easier condition, nor likely to accept our
rule in place of liberty; and the number is large, for a single
island, of cities of Hellenic origin. For except Naxos and
Catana, which I expect will side with us on account of their
kinship to the Leontines, there are seven others;[1] and these

[1] Syracuse, Selinus, Gela, Agrigentum, Messene, Himera,
Camarina (Schol.).

ἑπτά, καὶ παρεσκευασμέναι τοῖς πᾶσιν ὁμοιοτρόπως μάλιστα τῇ ἡμετέρᾳ δυνάμει, καὶ οὐχ ἥκιστα ἐπὶ ἃς
4 μᾶλλον πλέομεν, Σελινοῦς καὶ Συρακούσαι. πολλοὶ μὲν γὰρ ὁπλῖται ἔνεισι καὶ τοξόται καὶ ἀκοντισταί, πολλαὶ δὲ τριήρεις καὶ ὄχλος ὁ πληρώσων αὐτάς. χρήματά τ᾽ ἔχουσι, τὰ μὲν ἴδια, τὰ δὲ καὶ ἐν τοῖς ἱεροῖς ἔστι Σελινουντίοις· Συρακοσίοις δὲ καὶ ἀπὸ βαρβάρων τινῶν ἀπ᾽ ἀρχῆς φέρεται. ᾧ δὲ μάλιστα ἡμῶν προύχουσιν, ἵππους τε πολλοὺς κέκτηνται καὶ σίτῳ οἰκείῳ καὶ οὐκ ἐπακτῷ χρῶνται.

XXI. "Πρὸς οὖν τοιαύτην δύναμιν οὐ ναυτικῆς καὶ φαύλου στρατιᾶς μόνον δεῖ, ἀλλὰ καὶ πεζὸν πολὺν ξυμπλεῖν, εἴπερ βουλόμεθα ἄξιον τῆς διανοίας δρᾶν καὶ μὴ ὑπὸ ἱππέων πολλῶν εἴργεσθαι τῆς γῆς, ἄλλως τε καὶ εἰ ξυστῶσιν αἱ πόλεις φοβηθεῖσαι καὶ μὴ ἀντιπαράσχωσιν ἡμῖν φίλοι τινὲς γενόμενοι ἄλλοι
2 ἢ Ἐγεσταῖοι ᾧ ἀμυνούμεθα ἱππικόν· αἰσχρὸν δὲ βιασθέντας ἀπελθεῖν ἢ ὕστερον ἐπιμεταπέμπεσθαι τὸ πρῶτον ἀσκέπτως βουλευσαμένους. αὐτόθεν δὲ παρασκευῇ ἀξιόχρεῳ ἐπιέναι, γνόντας ὅτι πολύ τε ἀπὸ τῆς ἡμετέρας αὐτῶν μέλλομεν πλεῖν καὶ οὐκ ἐν τῷ ὁμοίῳ στρατευσόμενοι καὶ εἰ τοῖς τῇδε ὑπηκόοις ξύμμαχοι ἤλθετε ἐπί τινα, ὅθεν ῥᾴδιαι αἱ κομιδαὶ ἐκ τῆς φιλίας ὧν προσέδει, ἀλλὰ ἐς ἀλλοτρίαν πᾶσαν ἀπαρτήσαντες, ἐξ ἧς μηνῶν οὐδὲ τεσσάρων τῶν χειμερινῶν ἄγγελον ῥᾴδιον ἐλθεῖν.

are equipped with everything in a style very like to our own armament, and not least those against which our expedition is more immediately directed, Selinus and Syracuse. For they can supply many hoplites, archers and javelin-men, and possess many triremes and a multitude of men to man them. They have wealth, too, partly in private possession and partly in the temples at Selinus; and to the Syracusans tribute has come in from time immemorial from certain barbarians also; but their chief advantage over us is in the fact that they have many horses, and use grain that is home-grown and not imported.

XXI. "To cope with such a power we need not only a naval armament of such insignificant size, but also that a large force for use on land should accompany the expedition, if we would accomplish anything worthy of our design and not be shut out from the land by their numerous cavalry; especially if the cities become terrified and stand together, and some of the others, besides Egesta, do not become our friends and supply us cavalry with which to defend ourselves against that of the enemy. And it would be shameful to be forced to return home, or later to send for fresh supplies, because we had made our plans at first without due consideration. So we must start from home with an adequate armament, realizing that we are about to sail, not only far from our own land, but also on a campaign that will be carried on under no such conditions as if you had gone against an enemy as allies of your subject-states over here, where it would be easy to get whatever further supplies you needed from the friendly territory; nay, you will have removed into an utterly alien land, from which during the winter it is not easy for a messenger to come even in four months.

XXII. "Ὁπλίτας τε οὖν πολλούς μοι δοκεῖ χρῆναι
ἡμᾶς ἄγειν καὶ ἡμῶν αὐτῶν καὶ τῶν ξυμμάχων, τῶν τε
ὑπηκόων καὶ ἤν τινα ἐκ Πελοποννήσου δυνώμεθα ἢ
πεῖσαι ἢ μισθῷ προσαγαγέσθαι, καὶ τοξότας
πολλοὺς καὶ σφενδονήτας, ὅπως πρὸς τὸ ἐκείνων
ἱππικὸν ἀντέχωσι, ναυσί τε καὶ πολὺ περιεῖναι, ἵνα
καὶ τὰ ἐπιτήδεια ῥᾷον ἐσκομιζώμεθα, τὸν δὲ καὶ
αὐτόθεν σῖτον ἐν ὁλκάσι, πυροὺς καὶ πεφρυγμένας
κριθάς, ἄγειν καὶ σιτοποιοὺς ἐκ τῶν μυλώνων πρὸς
μέρος ἠναγκασμένους ἐμμίσθους, ἵνα, ἤν που ὑπὸ
ἀπλοίας ἀπολαμβανώμεθα, ἔχῃ ἡ στρατιὰ τὰ
ἐπιτήδεια (πολλὴ γὰρ οὖσα οὐ πάσης ἔσται πόλεως
ὑποδέξασθαι), τά τε ἄλλα ὅσον δυνατὸν ἑτοι-
μάσασθαι καὶ μὴ ἐπὶ ἑτέροις γίγνεσθαι, μάλιστα δὲ
χρήματα αὐτόθεν ὡς πλεῖστα ἔχειν. τὰ δὲ παρ'
Ἐγεσταίων, ἃ λέγεται ἐκεῖ ἕτοιμα, νομίσατε καὶ λόγῳ
ἂν μάλιστα ἕτοιμα εἶναι.

XXIII. "Ἢν γὰρ αὐτοὶ ἔλθωμεν ἐνθένδε μὴ
ἀντίπαλον μόνον παρασκευασάμενοι, πλήν γε πρὸς
τὸ μάχιμον αὐτῶν τὸ ὁπλιτικόν, ἀλλὰ καὶ
ὑπερβάλλοντες τοῖς πᾶσι, μόλις οὕτως οἷοί τε
2 ἐσόμεθα τῶν μὲν κρατεῖν, τὰ δὲ καὶ διασῶσαι. πόλιν
τε νομίσαι χρὴ ἐν ἀλλοφύλοις καὶ πολεμίοις
οἰκιοῦντας ἰέναι, οὓς πρέπει τῇ πρώτῃ ἡμέρᾳ ᾗ ἂν
κατάσχωσιν εὐθὺς κρατεῖν τῆς γῆς ἢ εἰδέναι ὅτι, ἢν
3 σφάλλωνται, πάντα πολέμια ἕξουσιν. ὅπερ ἐγὼ
φοβούμενος καὶ εἰδὼς πολλὰ μὲν ἡμᾶς δέον εὖ

XXII. "And so it seems to me that we ought to take hoplites in large numbers, both of our own and of our allies, and from our subjects, as well as any from the Peloponnesus that we can attract by pay or persuade; many bowmen, and also slingers, in order that they may withstand the cavalry of the enemy. And in ships we must have a decided superiority, in order that we may bring in our supplies more easily. And we must also take with us in merchantmen the grain in our stores here, wheat and parched barley, together with bakers requisitioned for pay from the mills in proportion to their size, in order that, if perchance we be detained by stress of weather, the army may have supplies. For the force will be large, and it will not be every city that can receive it. And all other things so far as possible we must get ready for ourselves, and not come to be at the mercy of the Siceliots; but we must especially have from here as much money as possible; for as to that of the Egestaeans, which is reported to be ready there, you may assume that it is indeed chiefly by report that it will ever be ready.

XXIII. "For if we go from here provided with an equipment of our own that is not only equal to theirs—except indeed as regards their fighting troops of heavy-armed men—but that even surpasses it in all respects, scarcely even so shall we be able to conquer Sicily or indeed to preserve our own army. It is, in fact, as you must believe, a city that we are going forth to found amid alien and hostile peoples, and it behooves men in such an enterprise to be at once, on the very day they land, masters of the soil, or at least to know that, if they fail in this, everything will be hostile to them. Fearing, then, this very result, and knowing that to succeed we must have been wise in planning to a

βουλεύσασθαι, ἔτι δὲ πλείω εὐτυχῆσαι, χαλεπὸν δὲ
ἀνθρώπους ὄντας, ὅτι ἐλάχιστα τῇ τύχῃ παραδοὺς
ἐμαυτὸν βούλομαι ἐκπλεῖν, παρασκευῇ δὲ ἀπὸ τῶν
4 εἰκότων ἀσφαλής. ταῦτα γὰρ τῇ τε ξυμπάσῃ πόλει
βεβαιότατα ἡγοῦμαι καὶ ἡμῖν τοῖς στρατευσομένοις
σωτήρια. εἰ δέ τῳ ἄλλως δοκεῖ, παρίημι αὐτῷ τὴν
ἀρχήν."

XXIV. Ὁ μὲν Νικίας τοσαῦτα εἶπε, νομίζων τοὺς
Ἀθηναίους τῷ πλήθει τῶν πραγμάτων ἢ ἀποτρέψειν ἤ,
εἰ ἀναγκάζοιτο στρατεύεσθαι, μάλιστ' ἂν οὕτως
2 ἀσφαλῶς ἐκπλεῦσαι. οἱ δὲ τὸ μὲν ἐπιθυμοῦν τοῦ πλοῦ
οὐκ ἐξῃρέθησαν ὑπὸ τοῦ ὀχλώδους τῆς παρασκευῆς,
πολὺ δὲ μᾶλλον ὥρμηντο καὶ τοὐναντίον περιέστη
αὐτῷ· εὖ τε γὰρ παραινέσαι ἔδοξε καὶ ἀσφάλεια νῦν
3 δὴ καὶ πολλὴ ἔσεσθαι. καὶ ἔρως ἐνέπεσε τοῖς πᾶσιν
ὁμοίως ἐκπλεῦσαι, τοῖς μὲν γὰρ πρεσβυτέροις ὡς ἢ
καταστρεψομένοις ἐφ' ἃ ἔπλεον ἢ οὐδὲν ἂν σφαλεῖσαν
μεγάλην δύναμιν, τοῖς δ' ἐν τῇ ἡλικίᾳ τῆς τε ἀπούσης
πόθῳ ὄψεως καὶ θεωρίας, καὶ εὐέλπιδες ὄντες
σωθήσεσθαι, ὁ δὲ πολὺς ὅμιλος καὶ στρατιώτης ἔν τε
τῷ παρόντι ἀργύριον οἴσειν καὶ προσκτήσεσθαι
4 δύναμιν ὅθεν ἀίδιον μισθοφορὰν ὑπάρξειν. ὥστε διὰ
τὴν ἄγαν τῶν πλειόνων ἐπιθυμίαν, εἴ τῳ ἄρα καὶ μὴ
ἤρεσκε, δεδιὼς μὴ ἀντιχειροτονῶν κακόνους δόξειεν
εἶναι τῇ πόλει ἡσυχίαν ἦγεν.

large extent, but to a still larger extent must have good fortune—a difficult thing, as we are but men—I wish, when I set sail, to have committed myself as little as possible to fortune, but so far as preparation is concerned to be, in all human probability, safe. For these precautions I regard as not only surest for the whole state but also as safeguards for us who are to go on the expedition. But if it seem otherwise to anyone, I yield the command to him."

XXIV. So much Nicias said, thinking that he would deter the Athenians by the multitude of his requirements, or, if he should be forced to make the expedition, he would in this way set out most safely. They, however, were not diverted from their eagerness for the voyage by reason of the burdensomeness of the equipment, but were far more bent upon it; and the result was just the opposite of what he had expected; for it seemed to them that he had given good advice, and that now certainly there would be abundant security. And upon all alike there fell an eager desire to sail—upon the elders, from a belief that they would either subdue the places they were sailing against, or that at any rate a great force could suffer no disaster; upon those in the flower of their age, through a longing for far-off sights and scenes, in good hopes as they were of a safe return; and upon the great multitude—that is, the soldiers—who hoped not only to get money for the present, but also to acquire additional dominion which would always be an inexhaustible source of pay. And so, on account of the exceeding eagerness of the majority, even if anyone was not satisfied, he held his peace, in the fear that if he voted in opposition he might seem to be disloyal to the state.

ARISTOPHANES

Translation by Jeffrey Henderson

ΛΥΣΙΣΤΡΑΤΗ
τοὺς πατέρας οὐ ποθεῖτε τοὺς τῶν παιδίων
100 ἐπὶ στρατιᾶς ἀπόντας; εὖ γὰρ οἶδ' ὅτι
πάσαισιν ὑμῖν ἐστιν ἀποδημῶν ἀνήρ.

ΚΑΛΟΝΙΚΗ
ὁ γοῦν ἐμὸς ἀνὴρ πέντε μῆνας, ὦ τάλαν,
ἄπεστιν ἐπὶ Θρᾴκης φυλάττων Εὐκράτη.

ΜΥΡΡΙΝΗ
ὁ δ' ἐμός γε τελέους ἑπτὰ μῆνας ἐν Πύλῳ.

ΛΑΜΠΙΤΩ
105 ὁ δ' ἐμός γα, καἴ κ' ἐκ τᾶς ταγᾶς ἔλσῃ ποκά,
πορπακισάμενος φροῦδος ἀμπτάμενος ἔβα.

ΚΑΛΟΝΙΚΗ
ἀλλ' οὐδὲ μοιχοῦ καταλέλειπται φεψάλυξ.
ἐξ οὗ γὰρ ἡμᾶς προὔδοσαν Μιλήσιοι,

Lysistrata 99–154

Athenian women decide to deny their husbands
sexual relations until they bring an end to
the war with Sparta

LYSISTRATA

Don't you all pine for your children's fathers when they're
off at war? I'm sure that every one of you has a husband
away from home.

CALONICE

My husband's been away five months, my dear, at the
Thracian front; he's guarding Eucrates.[14]

MYRRHINE

And mine's been at Pylos seven whole months.

LAMPITO

And mine, whenever he does come home from the regi-
ment, is soon strapping on his shield and flying off again.

CALONICE

Even lovers have vanished without a trace. Ever since
the Milesians revolted from us, I haven't even seen a six-

14 Substituting the name of an Athenian commander, not cer-
tainly identifiable, for the name of a city that the Athenians were
besieging.

ARISTOPHANES

οὐκ εἶδον οὐδ᾽ ὄλισβον ὀκτωδάκτυλον,
110 ὃς ἦν ἂν ἡμῖν σκυτίνη 'πικουρία.

ΛΥΣΙΣΤΡΑΤΗ

ἐθέλοιτ᾽ ἂν οὖν, εἰ μηχανὴν εὕροιμ᾽ ἐγώ,
μετ᾽ ἐμοῦ καταλῦσαι τὸν πόλεμον;

ΚΑΛΟΝΙΚΗ

νὴ τὼ θεὼ
ἐγὼ μὲν ἄν, κἂν εἴ με χρείη τοὔγκυκλον
τουτὶ καταθεῖσαν ἐκπιεῖν αὐθημερόν.

ΜΥΡΡΙΝΗ

115 ἐγὼ δέ γ᾽ ἄν, κἂν ὡσπερεὶ ψῆτταν δοκῶ
δοῦναι ἂν ἐμαυτῆς παρατεμοῦσα θἤμισυ.

ΛΑΜΠΙΤΩ

ἐγὼν δὲ καί κα ποττὸ Ταΰγετόν γ᾽ ἄνω
ἔλσοιμ᾽ ὅπᾳ μέλλοιμί γ᾽ εἰράναν ἰδῆν.

ΛΥΣΙΣΤΡΑΤΗ

λέγοιμ᾽ ἄν· οὐ δεῖ γὰρ κεκρύφθαι τὸν λόγον.
120 ἡμῖν γάρ, ὦ γυναῖκες, εἴπερ μέλλομεν
ἀναγκάσειν τοὺς ἄνδρας εἰρήνην ἄγειν,
ἀφεκτέ᾽ ἐστι—

ΚΑΛΟΝΙΚΗ

τοῦ; φράσον.

ΛΥΣΙΣΤΡΑΤΗ

ποιήσετ᾽ οὖν;

inch dildo, which might have been a consolation, however small.[15]

LYSISTRATA

Well, if I could devise a plan to end the war, would you be ready to join me?

CALONICE

By the Two Goddesses, I would, even if I had to pawn this dress and, on the very same day, drink up the proceeds!

MYRRHINE

As for me, I'd even cut myself in two like a flounder and donate half to the cause!

LAMPITO

And I would climb to the summit of Taygetus, if I could catch sight of peace from there.

LYSISTRATA

Here goes, then; no need to beat around the bush. Ladies, if we're going to force the men to make peace, we're going to have to give up—

CALONICE

Give up what? Tell us.

LYSISTRATA

You'll do it, then?

[15] Miletus, a notable exporter of dildoes (cf. fr. 592.16–28), had defected the previous summer (Thucydides 8.17).

ΚΑΛΟΝΙΚΗ

ποιήσομεν, κἂν ἀποθανεῖν ἡμᾶς δέῃ.

125

ΛΥΣΙΣΤΡΑΤΗ

ἀφεκτέα τοίνυν ἐστὶν ἡμῖν τοῦ πέους.
τί μοι μεταστρέφεσθε; ποῖ βαδίζετε;
αὗται, τί μοιμυᾶτε κἀνανεύετε;
τί χρὼς τέτραπται; τί δάκρυον κατείβεται;
ποιήσετ᾽ ἢ οὐ ποιήσετ᾽; ἢ τί μέλλετε;

ΚΑΛΟΝΙΚΗ

130   οὐκ ἂν ποιήσαιμ᾽, ἀλλ᾽ ὁ πόλεμος ἑρπέτω.

ΜΥΡΡΙΝΗ

μὰ Δί᾽ οὐδ᾽ ἐγὼ γάρ, ἀλλ᾽ ὁ πόλεμος ἑρπέτω.

ΛΥΣΙΣΤΡΑΤΗ

ταυτὶ σὺ λέγεις, ὦ ψῆττα; καὶ μὴν ἄρτι γε
ἔφησθα σαυτῆς κἂν παρατεμεῖν θἤμισυ.

ΚΑΛΟΝΙΚΗ

135   ἀλλ᾽, ἀλλ᾽ ὅ τι βούλει. κἂν με χρῇ, διὰ τοῦ πυρὸς
ἐθέλω βαδίζειν. τοῦτο μᾶλλον τοῦ πέους·
οὐδὲν γὰρ οἷον, ὦ φίλη Λυσιστράτη.

ΛΥΣΙΣΤΡΑΤΗ

τί δαὶ σύ;

ΓΥΝΗ Α´

κἀγὼ βούλομαι διὰ τοῦ πυρός.

ΛΥΣΙΣΤΡΑΤΗ

ὦ παγκατάπυγον θἠμέτερον ἅπαν γένος.
140   οὐκ ἐτὸς ἀφ᾽ ἡμῶν εἰσιν αἱ τραγῳδίαι·

CALONICE

We'll do it, even if it means our death!

LYSISTRATA

All right. We're going to have to give up—the prick. Why are you turning away from me? Where are you going? Why are you all pursing your lips and shaking your heads? What means your altered color and tearful droppings? Will you do it or not? What are you waiting for?

CALONICE

Count me out; let the war drag on.

MYRRHINE

Me too, by Zeus; let the war drag on.

LYSISTRATA

This from you, Ms. Flounder? Weren't you saying just a moment ago that you'd cut yourself in half?

CALONICE

Anything else you want, anything at all! I'm even ready to walk through fire; rather that than the prick. There's nothing like it, my dear Lysistrata.

LYSISTRATA

And what about you?

ATHENIAN WIFE

I'm ready to walk through fire too.

LYSISTRATA

Oh what a low and horny race are we! No wonder tragedies get written about us: we're nothing but Poseidon and a

οὐδὲν γάρ ἐσμεν πλὴν Ποσειδῶν καὶ σκάφη.
ἀλλ᾽, ὦ φίλη Λάκαινα,—σὺ γὰρ ἐὰν γένῃ
μόνη μετ᾽ ἐμοῦ, τὸ πρᾶγμ᾽ ἀνασωσαίμεσθ᾽ ἔτ᾽
    ⟨ἄν⟩—
ξυμψήφισαί μοι.

ΛΑΜΠΙΤΩ
            χαλεπὰ μὲν ναὶ τὼ σιὼ
γυναῖκας ὑπνῶν ἐστ᾽ ἄνευ ψωλᾶς μόνας.
145 ὅμως γα μάν· δεῖ τᾶς γὰρ εἰράνας μάλ᾽ αὖ.

ΛΥΣΙΣΤΡΑΤΗ
ὦ φιλτάτη σὺ καὶ μόνη τούτων γυνή.

ΚΑΛΟΝΙΚΗ
εἰ δ᾽ ὡς μάλιστ᾽ ἀπεχοίμεθ᾽ οὗ σὺ δὴ λέγεις,—
ὃ μὴ γένοιτο,—μᾶλλον ἂν διὰ τουτογὶ
γένοιτ᾽ ἂν εἰρήνη;

ΛΥΣΙΣΤΡΑΤΗ
150   πολύ γε νὴ τὼ θεώ.
εἰ γὰρ καθήμεθ᾽ ἔνδον ἐντετριμμέναι,
κἀν τοῖς χιτωνίοισι τοῖς ἀμοργίνοις
γυμναὶ παρίοιμεν δέλτα παρατετιλμέναι,
στύοιντο δ᾽ ἄνδρες κἀπιθυμοῖεν σπλεκοῦν,
ἡμεῖς δὲ μὴ προσίοιμεν, ἀλλ᾽ ἀπεχοίμεθα,
σπονδὰς ποιήσαιντ᾽ ἂν ταχέως, εὖ οἶδ᾽ ὅτι.

tub.[16] But my dear Spartan, if you alone would side with me, we might still salvage the plan; give me your vote!

LAMPITO
By the Twin Gods, it's difficult for females to sleep alone without the hard-on. But no matter, I assent; we need peace.

LYSISTRATA
You're an absolute dear, and the only real woman here!

CALONICE
Well, what if we did abstain from, uh, what you say, which heaven forbid: would peace be likelier to come on that account?

LYSISTRATA
Absolutely, by the Two Goddesses. If we sat around at home all made up, and walked past them wearing only our diaphanous underwear, with our pubes plucked in a neat triangle, and our husbands got hard and hankered to ball us, but we didn't go near them and kept away, they'd sue for peace, and pretty quick, you can count on that!

---

[16] In a myth twice dramatized by Sophocles, Tyro was seduced by the god Poseidon disguised as her lover, and exposed the resulting twin boys in a tub by the river.

XENOPHON

Translation by Carleton L. Brownson;
revised by John Dillery

2   I. Ἐπεὶ δὲ οἵ τε στρατηγοὶ συνειλημμένοι ἦσαν καὶ
τῶν λοχαγῶν καὶ τῶν στρατιωτῶν οἱ συνεπόμενοι
ἀπωλώλεσαν, ἐν πολλῇ δὴ ἀπορίᾳ ἦσαν οἱ Ἕλληνες,
ἐννοούμενοι ὅτι ἐπὶ ταῖς βασιλέως θύραις ἦσαν,
κύκλῳ δὲ αὐτοῖς πάντῃ πολλὰ καὶ ἔθνη καὶ πόλεις
πολέμιαι ἦσαν, ἀγορὰν δὲ οὐδεὶς ἔτι παρέξειν ἔμελ-
λεν, ἀπεῖχον δὲ τῆς Ἑλλάδος οὐ μεῖον ἢ μύρια στάδια,
ἡγεμὼν δ' οὐδεὶς τῆς ὁδοῦ ἦν, ποταμοὶ δὲ διεῖργον
ἀδιάβατοι ἐν μέσῳ τῆς οἴκαδε ὁδοῦ, προυδεδώκεσαν
δὲ αὐτοὺς καὶ οἱ σὺν Κύρῳ ἀναβάντες βάρβαροι,
μόνοι δὲ καταλελειμμένοι ἦσαν οὐδὲ ἱππέα οὐδένα
σύμμαχον ἔχοντες, ὥστε εὔδηλον ἦν ὅτι νικῶντες μὲν
οὐδ' ἂν ἕνα κατακάνοιεν, ἡττηθέντων δὲ αὐτῶν οὐδεὶς
3   ἂν λειφθείη· ταῦτα ἐννοούμενοι καὶ ἀθύμως ἔχοντες
ὀλίγοι μὲν αὐτῶν εἰς τὴν ἑσπέραν σίτου ἐγεύσαντο,
ὀλίγοι δὲ πῦρ ἀνέκαυσαν, ἐπὶ δὲ τὰ ὅπλα πολλοὶ οὐκ
ἦλθον ταύτην τὴν νύκτα, ἀνεπαύοντο δὲ ὅπου ἐτύγχα-
νεν ἕκαστος, οὐ δυνάμενοι καθεύδειν ὑπὸ λύπης καὶ

Anabasis 3.1.2–10

With the defeat of Cyrus 10,000 Greek mercenaries are
now stranded before the gates of Babylon; Xenophon
describes how he came to be among them

I. After the generals had been seized and such of the
captains and soldiers as accompanied them had been
killed, the Greeks were naturally in great perplexity, re-
flecting that they were at the King's gates, that round about
them on every side were many hostile tribes and cities,
that no one would provide them a market any longer, that
they were distant from Greece not less than ten thou-
sand stadia, that they had no guide to show them the way,
that they were cut off by impassable rivers which flowed
across the homeward route, that the barbarians who had
made the upward march with Cyrus had also betrayed
them, and that they were left alone, without even a single
horseman to support them, so that it was quite clear that
if they should be victorious, they could not kill anyone,
while if they should be defeated, not one of them would
be left alive. Full of these reflections and despondent as
they were, but few of them tasted food at evening, few
kindled a fire, and many did not come that night to their
quarters, but lay down wherever they each chanced to be,
unable to sleep for grief and longing for their native states

67

πόθου πατρίδων, γονέων, γυναικῶν, παίδων, οὓς οὔ-
ποτ᾽ ἐνόμιζον ἔτι ὄψεσθαι. οὕτω μὲν δὴ διακείμενοι
πάντες ἀνεπαύοντο.

4 Ἦν δέ τις ἐν τῇ στρατιᾷ Ξενοφῶν Ἀθηναῖος, ὃς
οὔτε στρατηγὸς οὔτε λοχαγὸς οὔτε στρατιώτης ὢν
συνηκολούθει, ἀλλὰ Πρόξενος αὐτὸν μετεπέμψατο οἴκ-
οθεν ξένος ὢν ἀρχαῖος· ὑπισχνεῖτο δὲ αὐτῷ, εἰ ἔλθοι,
φίλον αὐτὸν Κύρῳ ποιήσειν, ὃν αὐτὸς ἔφη κρείττω
5 ἑαυτῷ νομίζειν τῆς πατρίδος. ὁ μέντοι Ξενοφῶν ἀνα-
γνοὺς τὴν ἐπιστολὴν ἀνακοινοῦται Σωκράτει τῷ Ἀθη-
ναίῳ περὶ τῆς πορείας. καὶ ὁ Σωκράτης ὑποπτεύσας
μή τι πρὸς τῆς πόλεως ὑπαίτιον εἴη Κύρῳ φίλον
γενέσθαι, ὅτι ἐδόκει ὁ Κῦρος προθύμως τοῖς Λακεδαι-
μονίοις ἐπὶ τὰς Ἀθήνας συμπολεμῆσαι, συμβουλεύει
τῷ Ξενοφῶντι ἐλθόντα εἰς Δελφοὺς ἀνακοινῶσαι τῷ
6 θεῷ περὶ τῆς πορείας. ἐλθὼν δ᾽ ὁ Ξενοφῶν ἐπήρετο
τὸν Ἀπόλλω τίνι ἂν θεῶν θύων καὶ εὐχόμενος κάλλι-
στα καὶ ἄριστα ἔλθοι τὴν ὁδὸν ἣν ἐπινοεῖ καὶ καλῶς
πράξας σωθείη. καὶ ἀνεῖλεν αὐτῷ ὁ Ἀπόλλων θεοῖς
7 οἷς ἔδει θύειν. ἐπεὶ δὲ πάλιν ἦλθε, λέγει τὴν μαντείαν
τῷ Σωκράτει. ὁ δ᾽ ἀκούσας ᾐτιᾶτο αὐτὸν ὅτι οὐ τοῦτο
πρῶτον ἠρώτα πότερον λῷον εἴη αὐτῷ πορεύεσθαι ἢ
μένειν, ἀλλ᾽ αὐτὸς κρίνας ἰτέον εἶναι τοῦτ᾽ ἐπυνθάνετο
ὅπως ἂν κάλλιστα πορευθείη. ἐπεὶ μέντοι οὕτως ἤρου,
ταῦτ᾽, ἔφη, χρὴ ποιεῖν ὅσα ὁ θεὸς ἐκέλευσεν.

and parents, their wives and children, whom they thought they should never see again. Such was the state of mind in which they all lay down to rest.

There was a man in the army named Xenophon, an Athenian, who was neither general nor captain nor common soldier, but had accompanied the expedition because Proxenus, an old friend of his, had sent him at his home an invitation to go with him; Proxenus had also promised him that, if he would go, he would make him a friend of Cyrus, whom he himself regarded, so he said, as worth more to him than was his native state. After reading Proxenus' letter Xenophon conferred with Socrates, the Athenian, about the proposed journey; and Socrates, suspecting that his becoming a friend of Cyrus might be a cause for accusation against Xenophon on the part of the Athenian government, for the reason that Cyrus was thought to have given the Lacedaemonians zealous aid in their war against Athens, advised Xenophon to go to Delphi and consult the god in regard to this journey. So Xenophon went and asked Apollo to what one of the gods he should sacrifice and pray in order best and most successfully to perform the journey which he had in mind and, after meeting with good fortune, to return home in safety; and Apollo in his response told him to what gods he must sacrifice. When Xenophon came back from Delphi, he reported the oracle to Socrates; and upon hearing about it Socrates found fault with him because he did not first put the question whether it were better for him to go or stay, but decided for himself that he was to go and then asked the god as to the best way of going. "However," he added, "since you did put the question in that way, you must do all that the god directed."

8 Ὁ μὲν δὴ Ξενοφῶν οὕτω θυσάμενος οἷς ἀνεῖλεν ὁ
θεὸς ἐξέπλει, καὶ καταλαμβάνει ἐν Σάρδεσι Πρόξενον
καὶ Κῦρον μέλλοντας ἤδη ὁρμᾶν τὴν ἄνω ὁδόν, καὶ
9 συνεστάθη Κύρῳ. προθυμουμένου δὲ τοῦ Προξένου
καὶ ὁ Κῦρος συμπρουθυμεῖτο μεῖναι αὐτόν, εἶπε δὲ ὅτι
ἐπειδὰν τάχιστα ἡ στρατεία λήξῃ, εὐθὺς ἀποπέμψει
10 αὐτόν. ἐλέγετο δὲ ὁ στόλος εἶναι εἰς Πισίδας. ἐστρα-
τεύετο μὲν δὴ οὕτως ἐξαπατηθείς—οὐχ ὑπὸ Προξένου·
οὐ γὰρ ᾔδει τὴν ἐπὶ βασιλέα ὁρμὴν οὐδὲ ἄλλος οὐδεὶς
τῶν Ἑλλήνων πλὴν Κλεάρχου· ἐπεὶ μέντοι εἰς Κιλι-
κίαν ἦλθον, σαφὲς πᾶσιν ἤδη ἐδόκει εἶναι ὅτι ὁ στό-
λος εἴη ἐπὶ βασιλέα. φοβούμενοι δὲ τὴν ὁδὸν καὶ
ἄκοντες ὅμως οἱ πολλοὶ δι᾽ αἰσχύνην καὶ ἀλλήλων καὶ
Κύρου συνηκολούθησαν· ὧν εἷς καὶ Ξενοφῶν ἦν.

Xenophon, accordingly, after offering the sacrifices to the gods that Apollo's oracle prescribed, set sail, overtook Proxenus and Cyrus at Sardis as they were on the point of beginning the upward march, and was introduced to Cyrus. And not only did Proxenus urge him to stay with them, but Cyrus also joined in this request, adding that as soon as the campaign came to an end, he would send Xenophon home at once; and the report was that the campaign was against the Pisidians. It was in this way, then, that Xenophon came to go on the expedition, quite deceived about its purpose—not, however, by Proxenus, for he did not know that the attack was directed against the King, nor did anyone else among the Greeks with the exception of Clearchus; but by the time they reached Cilicia, it seemed clear to everybody that the expedition was really against the King. Then, although the Greeks were fearful of the journey and unwilling to go on, most of them did, nevertheless, out of shame before one another and before Cyrus, continue the march. And Xenophon was one of this number.

PLATO

Translation by Harold N. Fowler

3. ΦΑΙΔΩΝ. Ἐγώ σοι ἐξ ἀρχῆς πάντα πειρά-
σομαι διηγήσασθαι. ἀεὶ γὰρ δὴ καὶ τὰς πρόσθεν
D ἡμέρας εἰώθειμεν φοιτᾶν καὶ ἐγὼ καὶ οἱ ἄλλοι
παρὰ τὸν Σωκράτη, συλλεγόμενοι ἕωθεν εἰς τὸ
δικαστήριον, ἐν ᾧ καὶ ἡ δίκη ἐγένετο· πλησίον
γὰρ ἦν τοῦ δεσμωτηρίου. περιεμένομεν οὖν ἑκάστοτε,
ἕως ἀνοιχθείη τὸ δεσμωτήριον, διατρίβοντες
μετ᾽ ἀλλήλων· ἀνεῴγετο γὰρ οὐ πρῴ· ἐπειδὴ
δὲ ἀνοιχθείη, εἰσῇμεν παρὰ τὸν Σωκράτη καὶ
τὰ πολλὰ διημερεύομεν μετ᾽ αὐτοῦ. καὶ δὴ καὶ
τότε πρωιαίτερον συνελέγημεν. τῇ γὰρ προτεραίᾳ
E ἀπειδὴ ἀξύλθομεν ἄκ τοῦ δεσμωτηρίου ἀσπαρας,
ἐπυθόμεθα ὅτι τὸ πλοῖον ἐκ Δήλου ἀφιγμένον εἴη.
παρηγγείλαμεν οὖν ἀλλήλοις ἥκειν ὡς πρωιαίτατα
εἰς τὸ εἰωθός. καὶ ἥκομεν καὶ ἡμῖν ἐξελθὼν ὁ
θυρωρός, ὅσπερ εἰώθει ὑπακούειν, εἶπεν περιμένειν
καὶ μὴ πρότερον παριέναι, ἕως ἂν αὐτὸς κελεύσῃ.

72

Phaedo 3–5

Socrates with his friends on the day of his execution

PHAEDO. I will try to tell you everything from the beginning. On the previous days I and the others had always been in the habit of visiting Socrates. We used to meet at daybreak in the court where the trial took place, for it was near the prison ; and every day we used to wait about, talking with each other, until the prison was opened, for it was not opened early; and when it was opened, we went in to Socrates and passed most of the day with him. On that day we came together earlier; for the day before, when we left the prison in the evening we heard that the ship[1] had arrived from Delos. So we agreed to come to the usual place as early in the morning as possible. And we came, and the jailer who usually answered the door came out and told us to wait and not go in until he told us. "For," he said, "the

[1] A sacred ship; during its annual visit to Delos, executions were banned in Athens.

Λύουσι γάρ, ἔφη, οἱ ἕνδεκα Σωκράτη καὶ
παραγγέλλουσιν ὅπως ἂν τῇδε τῇ ἡμέρᾳ τελευτήσῃ.
οὐ πολὺν δ᾽ οὖν χρόνον ἐπισχὼν ἧκεν καὶ ἐκέλευεν
60 ἡμᾶς εἰσιέναι. εἰσελθόντες οὖν κατελαμβάνομεν τὸν
μὲν Σωκράτη ἄρτι λελυμένον, τὴν δὲ Ξανθίππην—
γιγνώσκεις γάρ—ἔχουσάν τε τὸ παιδίον αὐτοῦ καὶ
παρακαθημένην. ὡς οὖν εἶδεν ἡμᾶς ἡ Ξανθίππη,
ἀνευφήμησέ τε καὶ τοιαῦτ᾽ ἄττα εἶπεν, οἷα δὴ
εἰώθασιν αἱ γυναῖκες, ὅτι ῏Ω Σώκρατες, ὕστατον δή
σε προσεροῦσι νῦν οἱ ἐπιτήδειοι καὶ σὺ τούτους. καὶ ὁ
Σωκράτης βλέψας εἰς τὸν Κρίτωνα· ῏Ω Κρίτων, ἔφη,
ἀπαγέτω τις αὐτὴν οἴκαδε. καὶ ἐκείνην μὲν ἀπῆγόν
B τινες τῶν τοῦ Κρίτωνος βοῶσάν τε καὶ κοπτομένην·
ὁ δὲ Σωκράτης ἀνακαθιζόμενος εἰς τὴν κλίνην
συνέκαμψέ τε τὸ σκέλος καὶ ἐξέτριψε τῇ χειρί, καὶ
τρίβων ἅμα· Ὡς ἄτοπον, ἔφη, ὦ ἄνδρες, ἔοικέ τι εἶναι
τοῦτο, ὃ καλοῦσιν οἱ ἄνθρωποι ἡδύ· ὡς θαυμασίως
πέφυκε πρὸς τὸ δοκοῦν ἐναντίον εἶναι, τὸ λυπηρόν,
τῷ ἅμα μὲν αὐτὼ μὴ ἐθέλειν παραγίγνεσθαι τῷ
ἀνθρώπῳ, ἐὰν δέ τις διώκῃ τὸ ἕτερον καὶ λαμβάνῃ,
σχεδόν τι ἀναγκάζεσθαι λαμβάνειν καὶ τὸ ἕτερον,
ὥσπερ ἐκ μιᾶς κορυφῆς συνημμένω δύ᾽ ὄντε. καί μοι
C δοκεῖ, ἔφη, εἰ ἐνενόησεν αὐτὰ Αἴσωπος, μῦθον ἂν
συνθεῖναι, ὡς ὁ θεὸς βουλόμενος αὐτὰ διαλλάξαι
πολεμοῦντα, ἐπειδὴ οὐκ ἐδύνατο, συνῆψεν εἰς ταὐτὸν
αὐτοῖς τὰς κορυφάς, καὶ διὰ ταῦτα ᾧ ἂν τὸ ἕτερον
παραγένηται ἐπακολουθεῖ ὕστερον καὶ τὸ ἕτερον.

eleven are releasing Socrates from his fetters and giving directions how he is to die today." So after a little delay he came and told us to go in. We went in then and found Socrates just released from his fetters and Xanthippe—you know her—with his little son in her arms, sitting beside him. Now when Xanthippe saw us, she cried out and said the kind of thing that women always do say: "Oh Socrates, this is the last time now that your friends will speak to you or you to them." And Socrates glanced at Crito and said, "Crito, let somebody take her home." And some of Crito's people took her away wailing and beating her breast. But Socrates sat up on his couch and bent his leg and rubbed it with his hand, and while he was rubbing it, he said, "What a strange thing, my friends, that seems to be which men call pleasure! How wonderfully it is related to that which seems to be its opposite, pain, in that they will not both come to a man at the same time, and yet if he pursues the one and captures it, he is generally obliged to take the other also, as if the two were joined together in one head. And I think," he said, "if Aesop had thought of them, he would have made a fable telling how they were at war and god wished to reconcile them, and when he could not do that, he fastened their heads together, and for that reason, when one of them comes to anyone, the other follows after.

ὥσπερ οὖν καὶ αὐτῷ μοι ἔοικεν, ἐπειδὴ ὑπὸ τοῦ δεσμοῦ
ἦν ἐν τῷ σκέλει τὸ ἀλγεινόν, ἥκειν δὴ φαίνεται
ἐπακολουθοῦν τὸ ἡδύ.

4. Ὁ οὖν Κέβης ὑπολαβών· Νὴ τὸν Δία, ὦ
D Σώκρατες, ἔφη, εὖ γ᾽ ἐποίησας ἀναμνήσας με. περὶ
γάρ τοι τῶν ποιημάτων ὧν πεποίηκας ἐντείνας τοὺς
τοῦ Αἰσώπου λόγους καὶ τὸ εἰς τὸν Ἀπόλλω προοίμιον
καὶ ἄλλοι τινές με ἤδη ἤροντο, ἀτὰρ καὶ Εὔηνος
πρῴην, ὅ τι ποτὲ διανοηθείς, ἐπειδὴ δεῦρο ἦλθες,
ἐποίησας αὐτά, πρότερον οὐδὲν πώποτε ποιήσας. εἰ
οὖν τί σοι μέλει τοῦ ἔχειν ἐμὲ Εὐήνῳ ἀποκρίνασθαι,
ὅταν με αὖθις ἐρωτᾷ, εὖ οἶδα γάρ, ὅτι ἐρήσεται, εἰπέ,
τί χρὴ λέγειν. Λέγε τοίνυν, ἔφη, αὐτῷ, ὦ Κέβης,
τἀληθῆ, ὅτι οὐκ ἐκείνῳ βουλόμενος οὐδὲ τοῖς
E ποιήμασιν αὐτοῦ ἀντίτεχνος εἶναι ἐποίησα ταῦτα·
ᾔδειν γὰρ ὡς οὐ ῥᾴδιον εἴη· ἀλλ᾽ ἐνυπνίων τινῶν
ἀποπειρώμενος τί λέγει, καὶ ἀφοσιούμενος, εἰ
πολλάκις ταύτην τὴν μουσικήν μοι ἐπιτάττοι ποιεῖν.
ἦν γὰρ δὴ ἄττα τοιάδε· πολλάκις μοι φοιτῶν τὸ αὐτὸ
ἐνύπνιον ἐν τῷ παρελθόντι βίῳ, ἄλλοτ᾽ ἐν ἄλλῃ ὄψει
φαινόμενον, τὰ αὐτὰ δὲ λέγον, ὦ Σώκρατες, ἔφη,
μουσικὴν ποίει καὶ ἐργάζου. καὶ ἐγὼ ἔν γε τῷ πρόσθεν
χρόνῳ ὅπερ ἔπραττον τοῦτο ὑπελάμβανον αὐτό μοι
61 παρακελεύεσθαί τε καὶ ἐπικελεύειν, ὥσπερ οἱ τοῖς
θέουσι διακελευόμενοι, καὶ ἐμοὶ οὕτω τὸ ἐνύπνιον,
ὅπερ ἔπραττον, τοῦτο ἐπικελεύειν, μουσικὴν ποιεῖν, ὡς
φιλοσοφίας μὲν οὔσης μεγίστης μουσικῆς, ἐμοῦ δὲ

Just so it seems that in my case, after pain was in my leg on account of the fetter, pleasure appears to have come following after."

Here Cebes interrupted and said, "By Zeus, Socrates, I am glad you reminded me. Several others have asked about the poems you have composed, the metrical versions of Aesop's fables and the hymn to Apollo, and Evenus asked me the day before yesterday why you who never wrote any poetry before, composed these verses after you came to prison. Now, if you care that I should be able to answer Evenus when he asks me again—and I know he will ask me—tell me what to say."

"Then tell him, Cebes," said he, "the truth, that I composed these verses not because I wished to rival him or his poems, for I knew that would not be easy, but because I wished to test the meaning of certain dreams, and to make sure that I was neglecting no duty in case their repeated commands meant that I must cultivate the Muses in this way. They were something like this. The same dream came to me often in my past life, sometimes in one form and sometimes in another, but always saying the same thing: 'Socrates,' it said, 'make music and work at it.' And I formerly thought it was urging and encouraging me to do what I was doing already and that just as people encourage runners by cheering, so the dream was encouraging me to do what I was doing, that is, to make music, because philosophy was the greatest kind of music and I was working at

τοῦτο πράττοντος· νῦν δ' ἐπειδὴ ἥ τε δίκη ἐγένετο καὶ
ἡ τοῦ θεοῦ ἑορτὴ διεκώλυέ με ἀποθνῄσκειν, ἔδοξε
χρῆναι, εἰ ἄρα πολλάκις μοι προστάττοι τὸ ἐνύπνιον
ταύτην τὴν δημώδη μουσικὴν ποιεῖν, μὴ ἀπειθῆσαι
αὐτῷ, ἀλλὰ ποιεῖν. ἀσφαλέστερον γὰρ εἶναι μὴ
B ἀπιέναι πρὶν ἀφοσιώσασθαι ποιήσαντα ποιήματα
πειθόμενον τῷ ἐνυπνίῳ. οὕτω δὴ πρῶτον μὲν εἰς τὸν
θεὸν ἐποίησα, οὗ ἦν ἡ παροῦσα θυσία· μετὰ δὲ τὸν
θεόν, ἐννοήσας ὅτι τὸν ποιητὴν δέοι, εἴπερ μέλλοι
ποιητὴς εἶναι, ποιεῖν μύθους, ἀλλ' οὐ λόγους, καὶ
αὐτὸς οὐκ ἦ μυθολογικός, διὰ ταῦτα δὴ οὓς
προχείρους εἶχον καὶ ἠπιστάμην μύθους τοὺς
Αἰσώπου, τούτους ἐποίησα, οἷς πρώτοις ἐνέτυχον.

5. Ταῦτα οὖν, ὦ Κέβης, Εὐήνῳ φράζε, καὶ
ἐρρῶσθαι καί, ἂν σωφρονῇ, ἐμὲ διώκειν ὡς τάχιστα.
C ἄπειμι δέ, ὡς ἔοικε, τήμερον· κελεύουσι γὰρ Ἀθηναῖοι.

that. But now, after the trial and while the festival of the god delayed my execution, I thought, in case the repeated dream really meant to tell me to make this which is ordinarily called music, I ought to do so and not to disobey. For I thought it was safer not to go hence before making sure that I had done what I ought, by obeying the dream and composing verses. So first I composed a hymn to the god whose festival it was; and after the god, considering that a poet, if he is really to be a poet, must compose myths and not speeches, since I was not a maker of myths, I took the myths of Aesop, which I had at hand and knew, and turned into verse the first I came upon. So tell Evenus that, Cebes, and bid him farewell, and tell him, if he is wise, to come after me as quickly as he can. I, it seems, am going today; for that is the order of the Athenians."

ARISTOTLE

Translation by Stephen Halliwell

IV Ἐοίκασι δὲ γεννῆσαι μὲν ὅλως τὴν ποιητικὴν
αἰτίαι δύο τινὲς καὶ αὗται φυσικαί. τό τε γὰρ
5 μιμεῖσθαι σύμφυτον τοῖς ἀνθρώποις ἐκ παίδων ἐστὶ
καὶ τούτῳ διαφέρουσι τῶν ἄλλων ζῴων ὅτι
μιμητικώτατόν ἐστι καὶ τὰς μαθήσεις ποιεῖται διὰ
μιμήσεως τὰς πρώτας, καὶ τὸ χαίρειν τοῖς μιμήμασι
πάντας. σημεῖον δὲ τούτου τὸ συμβαῖνον ἐπὶ τῶν
10 ἔργων· ἃ γὰρ αὐτὰ λυπηρῶς ὁρῶμεν, τούτων τὰς
εἰκόνας τὰς μάλιστα ἠκριβωμένας χαίρομεν
θεωροῦντες, οἷον θηρίων τε μορφὰς τῶν ἀτιμοτάτων
καὶ νεκρῶν. αἴτιον δὲ καὶ τούτου, ὅτι μανθάνειν οὐ
μόνον τοῖς φιλοσόφοις ἥδιστον ἀλλὰ καὶ τοῖς ἄλλοις
ὁμοίως, ἀλλ᾽ ἐπὶ βραχὺ κοινωνοῦσιν αὐτοῦ. διὰ γὰρ
15 τοῦτο χαίρουσι τὰς εἰκόνας ὁρῶντες, ὅτι συμβαίνει
θεωροῦντας μανθάνειν καὶ συλλογίζεσθαι τί ἕκαστον,

80

Poetics 4
Origins and early development of
two branches of poetry

It can be seen that poetry was broadly engendered by a
pair of causes, both natural. For it is an instinct of human
beings, from childhood, to engage in mimesis (indeed, this
distinguishes them from other animals: man is the most
mimetic of all, and it is through mimesis that he develops
his earliest understanding); and equally natural that every-
one enjoys mimetic objects. A common occurrence indi-
cates this: we enjoy contemplating the most precise images
of things whose actual sight is painful to us, such as the
forms of the vilest animals and of corpses. The explanation
of this too is that understanding gives great pleasure not
only to philosophers but likewise to others too, though the
latter have a smaller share in it. This is why people enjoy
looking at images, because through contemplating them it
comes about that they understand and infer what each ele-
ment means, for instance that "this person is so-and-so."[1]

[1] I.e. in a portrait—a deliberately rudimentary instance of an
interpretative process which could take more complex forms.

οἷον ὅτι οὗτος ἐκεῖνος· ἐπεὶ ἐὰν μὴ τύχῃ προεωρακώς,
οὐχ ᾗ μίμημα ποιήσει τὴν ἡδονὴν ἀλλὰ διὰ τὴν
ἀπεργασίαν ἢ τὴν χροιὰν ἢ διὰ τοιαύτην τινὰ ἄλλην
αἰτίαν.

κατὰ φύσιν δὲ ὄντος ἡμῖν τοῦ μιμεῖσθαι καὶ τῆς
20 ἁρμονίας καὶ τοῦ ῥυθμοῦ (τὰ γὰρ μέτρα ὅτι μόρια τῶν
ῥυθμῶν ἐστι φανερὸν) ἐξ ἀρχῆς οἱ πεφυκότες πρὸς
αὐτὰ μάλιστα κατὰ μικρὸν προάγοντες ἐγέννησαν
τὴν ποίησιν ἐκ τῶν αὐτοσχεδιασμάτων. διεσπάσθη δὲ
κατὰ τὰ οἰκεῖα ἤθη ἡ ποίησις· οἱ μὲν γὰρ σεμνότεροι
25 τὰς καλὰς ἐμιμοῦντο πράξεις καὶ τὰς τῶν τοιούτων, οἱ
δὲ εὐτελέστεροι τὰς τῶν φαύλων, πρῶτον ψόγους
ποιοῦντες, ὥσπερ ἕτεροι ὕμνους καὶ ἐγκώμια. τῶν μὲν
οὖν πρὸ Ὁμήρου οὐδενὸς ἔχομεν εἰπεῖν τοιοῦτον
ποίημα, εἰκὸς δὲ εἶναι πολλούς, ἀπὸ δὲ Ὁμήρου
ἀρξαμένοις ἔστιν, οἷον ἐκείνου ὁ Μαργίτης καὶ τὰ
30 τοιαῦτα. ἐν οἷς κατὰ τὸ ἁρμόττον καὶ τὸ ἰαμβεῖον ἦλθε
μέτρον—διὸ καὶ ἰαμβεῖον καλεῖται νῦν, ὅτι ἐν τῷ
μέτρῳ τούτῳ ἰάμβιζον ἀλλήλους. καὶ ἐγένοντο τῶν
παλαιῶν οἱ μὲν ἡρωικῶν οἱ δὲ ἰάμβων ποιηταί. ὥσπερ
δὲ καὶ τὰ σπουδαῖα μάλιστα ποιητὴς Ὅμηρος ἦν
(μόνος γὰρ οὐχ ὅτι εὖ ἀλλὰ καὶ μιμήσεις δραματικὰς

For, if one happens not to have seen the subject before, the image will not give pleasure *qua* mimesis but because of its execution or colour, or for some other such reason.

Because mimesis comes naturally to us, as do melody and rhythm (that metres are categories of rhythms is obvious), in the earliest times[2] those with special natural talents for these things gradually progressed and brought poetry into being from improvisations. Poetry branched into two, according to its creators' characters: the more serious produced mimesis of noble actions and the actions of noble people, while the more vulgar depicted the actions of the base, in the first place by composing invectives[3] (just as others produced hymns and encomia).[4] Now, we cannot name such an invective by any poet earlier than Homer, though probably many poets produced them; but we can do so from Homer onwards, namely the latter's *Margites*[5] and the like. In these poems, it was aptness which brought the iambic metre too into use—precisely why it is called "iambic" now, because it was in this metre that they lampooned [*iambizein*] one another. Of the older poets some became composers of epic hexameters, others of iambic lampoons. Just as Homer was the supreme poet of elevated subjects (for he was preeminent not only in quality but also in composing dramatic mimesis), so too he

[2] Lit. "from the beginning": the point is *a priori* rather than strictly historical.

[3] Satirical lampoons on individuals.

[4] Poems in praise of gods and outstanding humans.

[5] A (lost) burlesque epic, named after its crass "hero," composed in a mixture of hexameters and iambic trimeters. It is not now, and was not always in antiquity, attributed to "Homer."

35 ἐποίησεν), οὕτως καὶ τὰ τῆς κωμῳδίας σχήματα
πρῶτος ὑπέδειξεν, οὐ ψόγον ἀλλὰ τὸ γελοῖον
δραματοποιήσας· ὁ γὰρ Μαργίτης ἀνάλογον ἔχει,
1449a ὥσπερ Ἰλιὰς καὶ ἡ Ὀδύσσεια πρὸς τὰς τραγῳδίας,
οὕτω καὶ οὗτος πρὸς τὰς κωμῳδίας. παραφανείσης δὲ
τῆς τραγῳδίας καὶ κωμῳδίας οἱ ἐφ' ἑκατέραν τὴν
ποίησιν ὁρμῶντες κατὰ τὴν οἰκείαν φύσιν οἱ μὲν
ἀντὶ τῶν ἰάμβων κωμῳδοποιοὶ ἐγένοντο, οἱ δὲ ἀντὶ
5 τῶν ἐπῶν τραγῳδοδιδάσκαλοι, διὰ τὸ μείζω καὶ
ἐντιμότερα τὰ σχήματα εἶναι ταῦτα ἐκείνων.

τὸ μὲν οὖν ἐπισκοπεῖν εἰ ἄρα ἔχει ἤδη ἡ τραγῳδία
τοῖς εἴδεσιν ἱκανῶς ἢ οὔ, αὐτό τε καθ' αὑτὸ κρῖναι
καὶ πρὸς τὰ θέατρα, ἄλλος λόγος. γενομένη δ' οὖν
ἀπ' ἀρχῆς αὐτοσχεδιαστικῆς (καὶ αὐτὴ καὶ ἡ
10 κωμῳδία, καὶ ἡ μὲν ἀπὸ τῶν ἐξαρχόντων τὸν
διθύραμβον, ἡ δὲ ἀπὸ τῶν τὰ φαλλικὰ ἃ ἔτι καὶ νῦν ἐν
πολλαῖς τῶν πόλεων διαμένει νομιζόμενα), κατὰ
μικρὸν ηὐξήθη προαγόντων ὅσον ἐγίγνετο φανερὸν
αὐτῆς· καὶ πολλὰς μεταβολὰς μεταβαλοῦσα ἡ
15 τραγῳδία ἐπαύσατο, ἐπεὶ ἔσχε τὴν αὑτῆς φύσιν. καὶ
τό τε τῶν ὑποκριτῶν πλῆθος ἐξ ἑνὸς εἰς δύο πρῶτος
Αἰσχύλος ἤγαγε καὶ τὰ τοῦ χοροῦ ἠλάττωσε καὶ τὸν

was the first to delineate the forms of comedy, by dramatising not invective but the laughable: thus *Margites* stands in the same relation to comedies as do the *Iliad* and *Odyssey* to tragedies. And when tragedy and comedy had been glimpsed,[6] those whose own natures gave them an impetus towards either type of poetry abandoned iambic lampoons to become comic poets, or epic to become tragedians, because these newer forms were grander and more esteemed[7] than the earlier.

To consider whether or not tragedy is even now sufficiently developed in its types—judging it intrinsically and in relation to audiences—is a separate matter. Anyhow, when it came into being from an improvisatory origin (that is, both tragedy and comedy: the former from the leaders of dithyramb, the other from the leaders of the phallic songs[8] which remain even now a custom in many cities), it was gradually enhanced as poets developed the potential they saw in it. And after going through many changes tragedy ceased to evolve, since it had achieved its own nature. Aeschylus innovated by raising the number of actors from one to two, reduced the choral component,[9]

6 I.e. potentially, within the nature of Homer's poetry.

7 This applies principally to Athens, and to creation of new works rather than abstract estimation of poems.

8 Sung to accompany processional carrying of phallic icons in ritual contexts; normally obscene and scurrilous: cf. Aristoph. *Ach.* 241–79.

9 Not consistently, as his surviving plays show, but in broad relation to his predecessors.

λόγον πρωταγωνιστεῖν παρεσκεύασεν· τρεῖς δὲ καὶ
σκηνογραφίαν Σοφοκλῆς. ἔτι δὲ τὸ μέγεθος· ἐκ
μικρῶν μύθων καὶ λέξεως γελοίας διὰ τὸ ἐκ σατυρικοῦ
20 μεταβαλεῖν ὀψὲ ἀπεσεμνύνθη, τό τε μέτρον ἐκ
τετραμέτρου ἰαμβεῖον ἐγένετο. τὸ μὲν γὰρ πρῶτον
τετραμέτρῳ ἐχρῶντο διὰ τὸ σατυρικὴν καὶ
ὀρχηστικωτέραν εἶναι τὴν ποίησιν, λέξεως δὲ
γενομένης αὐτὴ ἡ φύσις τὸ οἰκεῖον μέτρον εὗρε·
μάλιστα γὰρ λεκτικὸν τῶν μέτρων τὸ ἰαμβεῖόν ἐστιν·
25 σημεῖον δὲ τούτου, πλεῖστα γὰρ ἰαμβεῖα λέγομεν ἐν
τῇ διαλέκτῳ τῇ πρὸς ἀλλήλους, ἐξάμετρα δὲ ὀλιγάκις
καὶ ἐκβαίνοντες τῆς λεκτικῆς ἁρμονίας. ἔτι δὲ
ἐπεισοδίων πλήθη. καὶ τὰ ἄλλ᾽ ὡς ἕκαστα
κοσμηθῆναι λέγεται ἔστω ἡμῖν εἰρημένα· πολὺ γὰρ
30 ἂν ἴσως ἔργον εἴη διεξιέναι καθ᾽ ἕκαστον.

and made speech play the leading role. Three actors and scene painting came with Sophocles.[10] A further factor was grandeur: after a period of slight plots and laughable diction, owing to development from a satyric[11] ethos, it was at a late stage that tragedy acquired dignity, and its metre became the iambic trimeter instead of the trochaic tetrameter. To begin with they used the tetrameter because the poetry was satyric and more associated with dancing; but when spoken dialogue was introduced, tragedy's own nature discovered the appropriate metre. For the iambic trimeter, more than any other metre, has the rhythm of speech: an indication of this is that we speak many trimeters in conversation with one another, but hexameters only rarely and when diverging from the colloquial register. Further changes concerned the number of episodes. And we shall take as read the ways in which other features of tragedy are said to have been embellished; it would no doubt be a large task to discuss them individually.

[10] The third actor was probably introduced in the 460s, early in Soph.'s career; it is required in Aesch. *Oresteia* of 458. Scene painting: decoration of the stage building (*skene*), to give it an active dramatic status.

[11] I.e. with the tone of a satyr play. Did Ar. connect this tone with the early dithyrambs from which tragedy developed (49a10–11)?

CALLIMACHUS

Translation by A. W. Mair

οὔπω τὰν Κνιδίαν, ἔτι Δώτιον ἱρὸν ἔναιον,
25 τὶν δ' αὐτᾷ καλὸν ἄλσος ἐποιήσαντο Πελασγοὶ
    δένδρεσιν ἀμφιλαφές· διά κεν μόλις ἦνθεν ὀιστός·
    ἐν πίτυς, ἐν μεγάλαι πτελέαι ἔσαν, ἐν δὲ καὶ ὄχναι,
    ἐν δὲ καλὰ γλυκύμαλα· τὸ δ' ὥστ' ἀλέκτρινον ὕδωρ
    ἐξ ἀμαρᾶν ἀνέθυε. θεὰ δ' ἐπεμαίνετο χώρῳ
30 ὅσσον Ἐλευσῖνι, Τριόπῳ θ' ὅσον, ὁκκόσον Ἔννᾳ.
    ἀλλ' ὅκα Τριοπίδαισιν ὁ δεξιὸς ἄχθετο δαίμων,
    τουτάκις ἁ χείρων Ἐρυσίχθονος ἅψατο βωλά·
    σεύατ' ἔχων θεράποντας ἐείκοσι, πάντας ἐν ἀκμᾷ,
    πάντας δ' ἀνδρογίγαντας ὅλαν πόλιν ἀρκίος ἆραι,
35 ἀμφότερον πελέκεσσι καὶ ἀξίναισιν ὁπλίσσας,
    ἐς δὲ τὸ τᾶς Δάματρος ἀναιδέες ἔδραμον ἄλσος.
    ἧς δέ τις αἴγειρος, μέγα δένδρεον αἰθέρι κῦρον,

Hymns 6.24–117

In this hymn to Demeter Callimachus recounts
a sacrilege and its punishment

Not yet in the land of Cnidus, but still in holy Dotium
dwelt the Pelasgians and unto thyself they made a fair
grove abounding in trees; hardly would an arrow have
passed through them. Therein was pine, and therein were
mighty elms, and therein were pear-trees, and therein
were fair sweet-apples; and from the ditches gushed up
water as it were of amber. And the goddess[1] loved the place
to madness, even as Eleusis, as Triopum,[2] as Enna.[3]

But when their favouring fortune became wroth
with the Triopidae, then the worse counsel took hold of
Erysichthon.[4] He hastened with twenty attendants, all in
their prime, all men-giants able to lift a whole city, arming
them both with double axes and with hatchets, and they
rushed shameless into the grove of Demeter. Now there
was a poplar, a great tree reaching to the sky, and thereby

1 Demeter.
2 *i.e.* Triopium in Caria.
3 In Sicily.
4 Son of Triopas.

τῷ δ᾽ ἔπι ταὶ νύμφαι ποτὶ τῶνδιον ἐψιόωντο,
ἃ πράτα πλαγεῖσα κακὸν μέλος ἴαχεν ἄλλαις.
40 ἄσθετο Δαμάτηρ, ὅτι οἱ ξύλον ἱερὸν ἄλγει,
εἶπε δὲ χωσαμένα "τίς μοι καλὰ δένδρεα κόπτει;"
αὐτίκα Νικίππᾳ, τάν οἱ πόλις ἀράτειραν
δαμοσίαν ἔστασαν, ἐείσατο, γέντο δὲ χειρὶ
στέμματα καὶ μάκωνα, κατωμαδίαν δ᾽ ἔχε κλᾷδα.
45 φᾶ δὲ παραψύχοισα κακὸν καὶ ἀναιδέα φῶτα
"τέκνον, ὅτις τὰ θεοῖσιν ἀνειμένα δένδρεα κόπτεις,
τέκνον ἐλίνυσον, τέκνον πολύθεστε τοκεῦσι,
παύεο καὶ θεράποντας ἀπότρεπε, μή τι χαλεφθῇ
πότνια Δαμάτηρ, τᾶς ἱερὸν ἐκκεραΐζεις."
50 τὰν δ᾽ ἄρ᾽ ὑποβλέψας χαλεπώτερον ἠὲ κυναγὸν
ὤρεσιν ἐν Τμαρίοισιν ὑποβλέπει ἄνδρα λέαινα
ὠμοτόκος, τᾶς φαντὶ πέλειν βλοσυρώτατον ὄμμα,
"χάζευ," ἔφα, "μή τοι πέλεκυν μέγαν ἐν χροῒ πάξω.
ταῦτα δ᾽ ἐμὸν θησεῖ στεγανὸν δόμον, ᾧ ἔνι δαῖτας
55 αἰὲν ἐμοῖς ἑτάροισιν ἄδην θυμαρέας ἀξῶ."
εἶπεν ὁ παῖς, Νέμεσις δὲ κακὰν ἐγράψατο φωνάν.
Δαμάτηρ δ᾽ ἄφατόν τι κοτέσσατο, γείνατο δ᾽ ἁ
 θεύς·
ἴθματα μὲν χέρσω, κεφαλὰ δέ οἱ ἅψατ᾽ Ὀλύμπω.
οἱ μὲν ἄρ᾽ ἡμιθνῆτες, ἐπεὶ τὰν πότνιαν εἶδον,
60 ἐξαπίνας ἀπόρουσαν ἐνὶ δρυσὶ χαλκὸν ἀφέντες·
ἁ δ᾽ ἄλλως μὲν ἔασεν, ἀναγκαίᾳ γὰρ ἔποντο
δεσποτικὰν ὑπὸ χεῖρα, βαρὺν δ᾽ ἀπαμείψατ᾽ ἄνακτα
"ναὶ ναί, τεύχεο δῶμα, κύον, κύον, ᾧ ἔνι δαῖτας

the nymphs were wont to sport at noontide. This poplar was smitten first and cried a woeful cry to the others. Demeter marked that her holy tree was in pain, and she was angered and said: "Who cuts down my fair trees?" Straightway she likened her to Nicippe, whom the city had appointed to be her public priestess, and in her hand she grasped her fillets and her poppy, and from her shoulder hung her key. And she spake to soothe the wicked and shameless man and said: "My child, who cuttest down the trees which are dedicated to the gods, stay, my child, child of thy parents' many prayers, cease and turn back thine attendants, lest the lady Demeter be angered, whose holy place thou makest desolate." But with a look more fierce than that wherewith a lioness looks on the hunter on the hills of Tmarus—a lioness with new-born cubs, whose eye they say is of all most terrible—he said: "Give back, lest I fix my great axe in thy flesh! These trees shall make my tight dwelling wherein evermore I shall hold pleasing banquets enough for my companions." So spake the youth and Nemesis[5] recorded his evil speech. And Demeter was angered beyond telling and put on her goddess shape. Her steps touched the earth, but her head reached unto Olympus. And they, half-dead when they beheld the lady goddess, rushed suddenly away, leaving the bronze axes in the trees. And she left the others alone— for they followed by constraint beneath their master's hand—but she answered their angry king: "Yea, yea, build thy house, dog, dog, that

---

[5] Nemesis takes note of presumptuous acts and words, Plato, *Laws* 717 D.

ποιησεῖσ· θαμιναὶ γὰρ ἐς ὕστερον εἰλαπίναι τοι."
65 ἁ μὲν τόσσ' εἰποῖσ' Ἐρυσίχθονι τεῦχε πονηρά.
αὐτίκα οἱ χαλεπόν τε καὶ ἄγριον ἔμβαλε λιμὸν
αἴθωνα κρατερόν, μεγάλᾳ δ' ἐστρεύγετο νούσῳ.
σχέτλιος, ὅσσα πάσαιτο τόσων ἔχεν ἵμερος αὖτις.
εἴκατι δαῖτα πένοντο, δυώδεκα δ' οἶνον ἄφυσσον·
70 τόσσα Διώνυσον γὰρ ἃ καὶ Δάματρα χαλέπτει·
καὶ γὰρ τᾷ Δάματρι συνωργίσθη Διόνυσος.
οὔτε νιν εἰς ἐράνως οὔτε ξυνδείπνια πέμπον
αἰδόμενοι γονέες, προχανὰ δ' εὑρίσκετο πᾶσα.
ἦνθον Ἰτωνιάδος νιν Ἀθαναίας ἐπ' ἄεθλα
75 Ὀρμενίδαι καλέοντες· ἀπ' ὧν ἀρνήσατο μάτηρ
"οὐκ ἔνδοι, χθιζὸς γὰρ ἐπὶ Κραννῶνα βέβακε
τέλθος ἀπαιτησῶν ἑκατὸν βόας." ἦνθε Πολυξώ,
μάτηρ Ἀκτορίωνος, ἐπεὶ γάμον ἄρτυε παιδί,
ἀμφότερον Τριόπαν τε καὶ υἱέα κικλήσκοισα.
80 τὰν δὲ γυνὰ βαρύθυμος ἀμείβετο δάκρυ χέοισα
"νεῖταί τοι Τριόπας, Ἐρυσίχθονα δ' ἤλασε κάπρος
Πίνδον ἀν' εὐάγκειαν, ὁ δ' ἐννέα φάεα κεῖται."
δειλαία φιλότεκνε, τί δ' οὐκ ἐψεύσαο, μᾶτερ;
δαίννεν εἰλαπίναν τις· "ἐν ἀλλοτρίοις Ἐρυσίχθων."
85 ἄγετό τις νύμφαν· "Ἐρυσίχθονα δίσκος ἔτυψεν,"
ἢ "ἔπεσ' ἐξ ἵππων," ἢ "ἐν Ὄθρυϊ ποίμνι' ἀμιθρεῖ."
ἐνδόμυχος δήπειτα πανάμερος εἰλαπιναστὰς
ἤσθιε μυρία πάντα· κακὰ δ' ἐξάλλετο γαστὴρ
αἰεὶ μᾶλλος ἔδοντι, τὰ δ' ἐς βυθὸν οἷα θαλάσσας
90 ἀλεμάτως ἀχάριστα κατέρρεεν εἴδατα πάντα.

thou art, wherein thou shalt hold festival; for frequent banquets shall be thine hereafter." So much she said and devised evil things for Erysichthon. Straightway she sent on him a cruel and evil hunger—a burning hunger and a strong—and he was tormented by a grievous disease. Wretched man, as much as he ate, so much did he desire again. Twenty prepared the banquet for him, and twelve drew wine. For whatsoever things vex Demeter, vex also Dionysus; for Dionysus shares the anger of Demeter. His parents for shame sent him not to common feast or banquet, and all manner of excuse was devised. The sons of Ormenus[6] came to bid him to the games of Itonian Athene.[7] Then his mother refused the bidding: "He is not at home; for yesterday he is gone unto Crannon to demand a debt of a hundred oxen." Polyxo came, mother of Actorion—for she was preparing a marriage for her child—inviting both Triopas and his son. But the lady, heavy-hearted, answered with tears: "Triopas will come, but Erysichthon a boar wounded on Pindus of fair glens and he hath lain abed for nine days." Poor child-loving mother, what falsehood didst thou not tell ? One was giving a feast: "Erysichthon is abroad." One was bringing home a bride : "A quoit hath struck Erysichthon," or "he hath had a fall from his car," or "he is counting his flocks on Othrys.[8]" Then he within the house, an all-day banqueter, ate all things beyond reckoning. But his evil belly leaped all the more as he ate, and all the eatables poured, in vain and thanklessly, as it were into the depths of the sea. And even

6 Eponymous king of Ormenion in Thessaly.

7 So called from her cult at Itone in Thessaly.

8 Mountain in Thessaly.

ὡς δὲ Μίμαντι χιών, ὡς ἀελίῳ ἔνι πλαγγών,
καὶ τούτων ἔτι μεῖζον ἐτάκετο μέσφ᾽ ἐπὶ νευράς·
δειλαίῳ ἶνές τε καὶ ὀστέα μῶνον ἔλειφθεν.
κλαῖε μὲν ἁ μάτηρ, βαρὺ δ᾽ ἔστενον αἱ δύ᾽ ἀδελφαὶ
95 χὠ μαστὸς τὸν ἔπωνε καὶ αἱ δέκα πολλάκι δῶλαι.
καὶ δ᾽ αὐτὸς Τριόπας πολιαῖς ἐπὶ χεῖρας ἔβαλλε,
τοῖα τὸν οὐκ ἀίοντα Ποσειδάωνα καλιστρέων·
"ψευδοπάτωρ ἰδὲ τόνδε τεοῦ τρίτον, εἴπερ ἐγὼ μὲν
σεῦ τε καὶ Αἰολίδος Κανάκας γένος, αὐτὰρ ἐμεῖο
100 τοῦτο τὸ δείλαιον γένετο βρέφος· αἴθε γὰρ αὐτὸν
βλητὸν ὑπ᾽ Ἀπόλλωνος ἐμαὶ χέρες ἐκτερέιξαν·
νῦν δὲ κακὰ βούβρωστις ἐν ὀφθαλμοῖσι κάθηται.
ἤ οἱ ἀπόστασον χαλεπὰν νόσον ἠέ νιν αὐτὸς
βόσκε λαβών· ἁμαὶ γὰρ ἀπειρήκαντι τράπεζαι.
105 χῆραι μὲν μάνδραι, κεναὶ δέ μοι αὔλιες ἤδη
τετραπόδων, ἤδη γὰρ ἀπαρνήσαντο μάγειροι."
    ἀλλὰ καὶ οὐρῆας μεγαλᾶν ὑπέλυσαν ἀμαξᾶν,
καὶ τὰν βῶν ἔφαγεν, τὰν Ἑστίᾳ ἔτρεφε μάτηρ,
καὶ τὸν ἀεθλοφόρον καὶ τὸν πολεμήιον ἵππον,
110 καὶ τὰν αἴλουρον, τὰν ἔτρεμε θηρία μικκά.
    μέσφ᾽ ὄκα μὲν Τριόπαο δόμοις ἔνι χρήματα κεῖτο,
μῶνοι ἄρ᾽ οἰκεῖοι θάλαμοι κακὸν ἠπίσταντο.
ἀλλ᾽ ὄκα τὸν βαθὺν οἶκον ἀνεξήραναν ὀδόντες,
καὶ τόχ᾽ ὁ τῶ βασιλῆος ἐνὶ τριόδοισι καθῆστο
115 αἰτίζων ἀκόλως τε καὶ ἔκβολα λύματα δαιτός.
Δάματερ, μὴ τῆνος ἐμὶν φίλος, ὅς τοι ἀπεχθής,
εἴη μηδ᾽ ὁμότοιχος· ἐμοὶ κακογείτονες ἐχθροί.

as the snow upon Mimas, as a wax doll in the sun, yea, even more than these he wasted to the very sinews: only sinews and bones had the poor man left. His mother wept, and greatly groaned his two sisters, and the breast that suckled him and the ten handmaidens over and over. And Triopas himself laid hands on his grey hairs, calling on Poseidon, who heeded not, with such words as these: "False father, behold this the third generation of thy sons—if I am son of thee and of Canace, daughter of Aeolus, and this hapless child is mine. Would that he had been smitten by Apollo and that my hands had buried him! But now he sits an accursed glutton before mine eyes. Either do thou remove from him his cruel disease or take and feed him thyself; for my tables are already exhausted. Desolate are my folds and empty my byres of four-footed beasts; for already the cooks have said me "no."

But even the mules they loosed from the great wains and he ate the heifer that his mother was feeding for Hestia[9] and the racing horse and the war charger, and the cat at which the little vermin trembled.

So long as there were stores in the house of Triopas, only the chambers of the house were aware of the evil thing; but when his teeth dried up the rich house, then the king's son sat at the crossways, begging for crusts and the cast out refuse of the feast. O Demeter, never may that man be my friend who is hateful to thee, nor ever may he share party-wall with me; ill neighbours I abhor.

[9] At libations and sacrifices the first and last offerings were made to Hestia, the goddess of the family hearth.

JOSEPHUS

Translation by H. St. J. Thackeray

280   (3) Πέτραν οὐκ ὀλίγην τῇ περιόδῳ καὶ μῆκος
ὑψηλὴν πανταχόθεν περιερρώγασι βαθεῖαι φάραγ-
γες, κάτωθεν ἐξ ἀοράτου τέρματος κρημνώδεις
καὶ πάσῃ βάσει ζῴων ἀπρόσιτοι, πλὴν ὅσον κατὰ
δύο τόπους τῆς πέτρας εἰς ἄνοδον οὐκ εὐμαρῆ
281   παρεικούσης. ἔστι δὲ τῶν ὁδῶν ἡ μὲν ἀπὸ τῆς
Ἀσφαλτίτιδος λίμνης πρὸς ἥλιον ἀνίσχοντα, καὶ
πάλιν ἀπὸ τῆς δύσεως ᾗ ῥᾷον πορευθῆναι. καλοῦσι
282   δὲ ἣν ἑτέραν ὄφιν, τῇ στενότητι προσεικάσαντες καὶ
τοῖς συνεχέσιν ἑλιγμοῖς· κλᾶται γὰρ περὶ τὰς τῶν
κρημνῶν ἐξοχὰς καὶ πολλάκις εἰς αὐτὴν ἀνατρέχουσα
καὶ κατὰ μικρὸν αὖθις ἐκμηκυνομένη μόλις ψαύει τοῦ
283   πρόσω. δεῖ δὲ παραλλὰξ τὸν δι᾽ αὐτῆς βαδίζοντα
τὸν ἕτερον τῶν ποδῶν ἐρείδεσθαι. ἔστι δὲ πρόδηλος
ὄλεθρος· ἑκατέρωθεν γὰρ βάθος κρημνῶν ὑποκέχηνε
τῇ φοβερότητι πᾶσαν εὐτολμίαν ἐκπλῆξαι δυνάμενον.
284   διὰ τοιαύτης οὖν ἐλθόντι σταδίους τριάκοντα κορυφὴ

Jewish War 7.280–303

Herod's fortified palace at Masada

(3) A rock of no slight circumference and lofty from end to end is abruptly terminated on every side by deep ravines, the precipices rising sheer from an invisible base and being inaccessible to the foot of any living creature, save in two places where the rock permits of no easy ascent. Of these tracks one leads from the Lake Asphaltitis[1] on the east,[2] the other, by which the approach is easier, from the west. The former they call the snake, seeing a resemblance to that reptile in its narrowness and continual windings; for its course is broken in skirting the jutting crags and, returning frequently upon itself and gradually lengthening out again, it makes painful headway. One traversing this route must firmly plant each foot alternately. Destruction faces him; for on either side yawn chasms so terrific as to daunt the hardiest. After following this perilous track for thirty furlongs, one reaches the summit,

[1] The Dead Sea.
[2] Literally "towards the sun-rising," a phrase found in Herodotus (iii. 98).

τὸ λοιπόν ἐστιν, οὐκ εἰς ὀξὺ τέρμα συνηγμένη, ἀλλ'
285 ὥστ' εἶναι κατ' ἄκρας ἐπίπεδον. ἐπὶ ταύτῃ πρῶτον μὲν
ὁ ἀρχιερεὺς ᾠκοδομήσατο φρούριον Ἰωνάθης καὶ
προσηγόρευσε Μασάδαν, ὕστερον δ' Ἡρώδῃ τῷ
βασιλεῖ διὰ πολλῆς ἐγένετο σπουδῆς ἡ τοῦ χωρίου
286 κατασκευή. τεῖχός τε γὰρ ἤγειρε περὶ πάντα τὸν
κύκλον τῆς κορυφῆς ἑπτὰ σταδίων ὄντα, λευκοῦ μὲν
λίθου πεποιημένον, ὕψος δὲ δώδεκα καὶ πλάτος ὀκτὼ
287 πήχεις ἔχον, τριάκοντα δ' αὐτῷ καὶ ἑπτὰ πύργοι
πεντηκονταπήχεις ἀνειστήκεσαν, ἐξ ὧν ἦν εἰς
οἰκήματα διελθεῖν περὶ πᾶν τὸ τεῖχος ἔνδον
288 ᾠκοδομημένα. τὴν γὰρ κορυφὴν πίονα καὶ πεδίου
παντὸς οὖσαν μαλακωτέραν ἀνῆκεν εἰς γεωργίαν ὁ
βασιλεύς, ἵν' εἴ ποτε τῆς ἔξωθεν τροφῆς ἀπορία
γένοιτο, μηδὲ ταύτῃ κάμοιεν οἱ τὴν αὑτῶν σωτηρίαν
289 τῷ φρουρίῳ πεπιστευκότες. καὶ βασίλειον δὲ
κατεσκεύασεν ἐν αὐτῷ κατὰ τὴν ἀπὸ τῆς ἑσπέρας
ἀνάβασιν, ὑποκάτω μὲν τῶν τῆς ἄκρας τειχῶν,
πρὸς δὲ τὴν ἄρκτον ἐκκλίνον. τοῦ δὲ βασιλείου τὸ
τεῖχος ἦν ὕψει μέγα καὶ καρτερόν, πύργους ἔχον
290 ἑξηκονταπήχεις ἐγγωνίους τέτταρας. ἥ τε τῶν
οἰκημάτων ἔνδον καὶ στοῶν καὶ βαλανείων κατασκευὴ
παντοία καὶ πολυτελὴς ἦν, κιόνων μὲν ἁπανταχοῦ
μονολίθων ὑφεστηκότων, τοίχων δὲ καὶ τῶν ἐν τοῖς
οἰκήμασιν ἐδάφων λίθου στρώσει πεποικιλμένων.
291 πρὸς ἕκαστον δὲ τῶν οἰκουμένων τόπων ἄνω τε καὶ
περὶ τὸ βασίλειον καὶ πρὸ τοῦ τείχους πολλοὺς καὶ
μεγάλους ἐτετμήκει λάκκους ἐν ταῖς πέτραις

which, instead of tapering to a sharp peak, expands into a plain. On this plateau the high priest Jonathan[3] first erected a fortress and called it Masada; the subsequent planning of the place engaged the serious attention of King Herod. For first he enclosed the entire summit, a circuit measuring seven furlongs, with a wall of white stone, twelve cubits high and eight broad; on it stood thirty-seven towers, fifty cubits high, from which access was obtained to apartments constructed round the whole interior of the wall. For the actual top, being of rich soil and softer than any plain, was given up by the king to cultivation; in order that, should there ever be a dearth of provisions from outside, those who had committed their lives to the protection of the fortress might not suffer from it. There, too, he built a palace on the western slope, beneath the ramparts on the crest and inclining towards the north. The palace wall was strong and of great height, and had four towers, sixty cubits high, at the corners. The fittings of the interior—apartments, colonnades, and baths—were of manifold variety and sumptuous; columns, each formed of a single block, supporting the building throughout, and the walls and floors of the apartments being laid with variegated stones. Moreover, at each spot used for habitation, both on the summit and about the palace, as also before the wall, he had cut out in the rock numerous large tanks,

---

[3] Brother of Judas Maccabaeus and his successor as Jewish leader, 161–143 B.C.

φυλακτῆρας ὑδάτων, μηχανώμενος εἶναι χορηγίαν
292 ὅση τῷ ἐκ πηγῶν ἐστι χρωμένοις. ὀρυκτὴ δ᾽ ὁδὸς ἐκ
τοῦ βασιλείου πρὸς ἄκραν τὴν κορυφὴν ἀνέφερε τοῖς
ἔξωθεν ἀφανής. οὐ μὴν οὐδὲ ταῖς φανεραῖς ὁδοῖς ἦν
293 οἷόν τε χρήσασθαι ῥᾳδίως πολεμίοις· ἡ μὲν γὰρ ἑῴα
διὰ τὴν φύσιν, ὡς προείπαμεν, ἐστὶν ἄβατος, τὴν δ᾽
ἀπὸ τῆς ἑσπέρας μεγάλῳ κατὰ τὸ στενότατον πύργῳ
διετείχισεν, ἀπέχοντι τῆς ἄκρας πήχεων οὐκ ἔλαττον
διάστημα χιλίων, ὃν οὔτε παρελθεῖν δυνατὸν ἦν οὔτε
ῥᾴδιον ἑλεῖν· δυσέξοδος δὲ καὶ τοῖς μετὰ ἀδείας
294 βαδίζουσιν ἐπεποίητο. οὕτως μὲν οὖν πρὸς τὰς τῶν
πολεμίων ἐφόδους φύσει τε καὶ χειροποιήτως τὸ
φρούριον ὠχύρωτο.

295　(4) Τῶν δ᾽ ἔνδον ἀποκειμένων παρασκευῶν ἔτι
μᾶλλον ἄν τις ἐθαύμασε τὴν λαμπρότητα καὶ τὴν
296 διαμονήν· σῖτός τε γὰρ ἀπέκειτο πολὺς καὶ πολὺν
χρόνον ἀρκεῖν ἱκανώτατος οἶνός τε πολὺς ἦν καὶ
ἔλαιον, ἔτι δὲ παντοῖος ὀσπρίων καρπὸς καὶ φοίνικες
297 ἐσεσώρευντο. πάντα δ᾽ εὗρεν ὁ Ἐλεάζαρος τοῦ
φρουρίου μετὰ τῶν σικαρίων ἐγκρατὴς δόλῳ
γενόμενος ἀκμαῖα καὶ μηδὲν τῶν νεωστὶ κειμένων
ἀποδέοντα· καίτοι σχεδὸν ἀπὸ τῆς παρασκευῆς εἰς
τὴν ὑπὸ Ῥωμαίοις ἅλωσιν ἑκατὸν ἦν χρόνος ἐτῶν·
ἀλλὰ καὶ Ῥωμαῖοι τοὺς περιλειφθέντας τῶν καρπῶν
298 εὗρον ἀδιαφθόρους. αἴτιον δ᾽ οὐκ ἂν ἁμάρτοι τις
ὑπολαμβάνων εἶναι τὸν ἀέρα τῆς διαμονῆς, ὕψει τῶν
περὶ τὴν ἄκραν πάσης ὄντα γεώδους καὶ θολερᾶς
299 ἀμιγῆ κράσεως. εὑρέθη δὲ καὶ παντοίων πλῆθος

100

as reservoirs for water, thus procuring a supply as ample as where springs are available. A sunk road led up from the palace to the summit of the hill, imperceptible from without. But even of the open approaches it was not easy for an enemy to make use; for the eastern track, as we have previously stated, is from its nature impracticable, while that on the west Herod barred at its narrowest point by a great tower, distant no less than a thousand cubits from the crest. This tower it was neither possible to pass nor easy to capture; exit being rendered difficult even for passengers who had no cause for alarm. So strongly had this fortress been intrenched against an enemy's attack, both by nature and the hand of man.

(4) But the stores laid up within would have excited still more amazement, alike for their lavish splendour and their durability. For here had been stored a mass of corn, amply sufficient to last for years, abundance of wine and oil, besides every variety of pulse and piles of dates. All these Eleazar, when he with his Sicarii became through treachery master of the fortress, found in perfect condition and no whit inferior to goods recently laid in; although from the date of storage to the capture of the place by the Romans well-nigh a century had elapsed.[4] Indeed, the Romans found what remained of the fruits undecayed. It would not be erroneous to attribute such durability to the atmosphere, which at the altitude of the citadel is untainted by all earth-born and foul alloy. There was also

[4] If the fortress was stocked in Cleopatra's lifetime (§ 300), upward of a century had elapsed, from before 31 B.C. to A.D. 73.

ὅπλων ὑπὸ τοῦ βασιλέως ἀποτεθησαυρισμένον, ὡς
ἀνδράσιν ἀρκεῖν μυρίοις, ἀργός τε σίδηρος καὶ
χαλκὸς ἔτι δὲ καὶ μόλιβος, ἅτε δὴ τῆς παρασκευῆς ἐπὶ
300 μεγάλαις αἰτίαις γενομένης· λέγεται γὰρ αὐτῷ τὸν
Ἡρώδην τοῦτο τὸ φρούριον εἰς ὑποφυγὴν ἑτοιμάζειν
διπλοῦν ὑφορώμενον κίνδυνον, τὸν μὲν παρὰ τοῦ
πλήθους τῶν Ἰουδαίων, μὴ καταλύσαντες ἐκεῖνον τοὺς
πρὸ αὐτοῦ βασιλέας ἐπὶ τὴν ἀρχὴν καταγάγωσι, τὸν
μείζω δὲ καὶ χαλεπώτερον ἐκ τῆς βασιλευούσης
301 Αἰγύπτου Κλεοπάτρας. αὕτη γὰρ τὴν αὑτῆς γνώμην
οὐκ ἐπεῖχεν, ἀλλὰ πολλάκις Ἀντωνίῳ λόγους
προσέφερε, τὸν μὲν Ἡρώδην ἀνελεῖν ἀξιοῦσα,
χαρίσασθαι δ' αὐτῇ τὴν βασιλείαν τῶν Ἰουδαίων
302 δεομένη. καὶ μᾶλλον ἄν τις ἐθαύμασεν ὅτι μηδέπω
τοῖς προστάγμασιν Ἀντώνιος ὑπακήκοει, κακῶς ὑπὸ
τοῦ πρὸς αὐτὴν ἔρωτος δεδουλωμένος, οὐχ ὅτι περὶ
303 τοῦ μὴ χαρίσασθαι προσεδόκησεν. διὰ τοιούτους μὲν
φόβους Ἡρώδης Μασάδαν κατεσκευασμένος ἔμελλεν
Ῥωμαίοις ἀπολείψειν ἔργον τοῦ πρὸς Ἰουδαίους
πολέμου τελευταῖον.

found a mass of arms of every description, hoarded up by the king and sufficient for ten thousand men, besides unwrought iron, brass, and lead; these preparations having, in fact, been made for grave reasons. For it is said that Herod furnished this fortress as a refuge for himself, suspecting a twofold danger: peril on the one hand from the Jewish people, lest they should depose him and restore their former dynasty to power; the greater and more serious from Cleopatra, queen of Egypt. For she never concealed her intention, but was constantly importuning Antony, urging him to slay Herod, and praying him to confer on her the throne of Judaea. And, far from expecting him to refuse to gratify her, one might rather be surprised that Antony should never have obeyed her behests, basely enslaved as he was by his passion for her. It was such fears that drove Herod to fortify Masada, which he was destined to leave to the Romans as a final task in their war with the Jews.

PLUTARCH

Translation by Bernadotte Perrin

IV. Ἐπεὶ δὲ τὰ πράγματα διέστη Πομπηΐου καὶ
Καίσαρος ἐξενεγκαμένων τὰ ὅπλα καὶ τῆς ἡγεμονίας
ταραχθείσης, ἐπίδοξος μὲν ἦν αἱρήσεσθαι τὰ
Καίσαρος· ὁ γὰρ πατὴρ αὐτοῦ διὰ τὸν Πομπήϊον
2 ἐτεθνήκει πρότερον· ἀξιῶν δὲ τὰ κοινὰ τῶν ἰδίων
ἐπίπροσθεν ποιεῖσθαι καὶ τὴν Πομπηΐου νομίζων
ὑπόθεσιν βελτίονα πρὸς τὸν πόλεμον εἶναι τῆς
3 τοῦ Καίσαρος ἐκείνῳ προσέθετο. καίτοι πρότερον
ἀπαντήσας οὐδὲ προσεῖπε τὸν Πομπήϊον, ἄγος
ἡγούμενος μέγα πατρὸς φονεῖ διαλέγεσθαι· τότε δ' ὡς
ἄρχοντι τῆς πατρίδος ὑποτάξας ἑαυτὸν εἰς Κιλικίαν
ἔπλευσε πρεσβευτὴς μετὰ Σηστίου τοῦ λαχόντος τὴν
4 ἐπαρχίαν. ὡς δ' ἐκεῖ πράττειν οὐδὲν ἦν μέγα καὶ
συνῄεσαν εἰς ταὐτὸ ἤδη Πομπήϊος καὶ Καίσαρ
ἀγωνιζόμενοι περὶ τῶν ὅλων, ἧκεν εἰς Μακεδονίαν
5 ἐθελοντὴς τοῦ κινδύνου μεθέξων· ὅτε καί φασι
Πομπήϊον ἡσθέντα καὶ θαυμάσαντα προσιόντος
αὐτοῦ καθεζόμενον ἐξαναστῆναι καὶ περιβαλεῖν
104

Brutus 4–6

Examples of Brutus' nobility of character

IV. Here, when the state was rent by factions, Pompey and Caesar appealing to arms and the supreme power being confounded, Brutus was expected to choose the side of Caesar, since his father had been put to death a while before at the instigation of Pompey; but thinking it his duty to put the public good above his own, and holding that Pompey's grounds for going to war were better than Caesar's, he attached himself to Pompey. And yet before this he would not even speak to Pompey when he met him, considering it a great abomination to converse with the murderer of his father; now, however, looking upon him as his country's ruler, he put himself under his orders, and set sail for Cilicia as legate with Sestius, to whom the province had been allotted. But since there was nothing of importance for him to do there, and since Pompey and Caesar were now about to meet in a supreme struggle, he came of his own accord into Macedonia to share the danger. It was then, they say, that Pompey was so filled with delight and admiration that he rose from his seat as Brutus approached, and in the sight of all embraced him as a supe-

6 ὡς κρείττονα πάντων ὁρώντων. ἐν δὲ τῇ στρατείᾳ
τῆς ἡμέρας ὅσα μὴ Πομπηΐῳ συνῆν περὶ λόγους
καὶ βιβλία διέτριβεν, οὐ μόνον τὸν ἄλλον χρόνον,
7 ἀλλὰ καὶ πρὸ τῆς μεγάλης μάχης. ἦν μὲν ἀκμὴ
θέρους καὶ καῦμα πολὺ πρὸς ἑλώδεσι χωρίοις
ἐστρατοπεδευκότων, τῷ δὲ Βρούτῳ οὐ ταχέως ἦκον οἱ
8 τὴν σκηνὴν κομίζοντες. ἐκπονηθεὶς δὲ περὶ ταῦτα,
μεσημβρίας μόλις ἀλειψάμενος καὶ φαγὼν ὀλίγα, τῶν
ἄλλων ἢ καθευδόντων ἢ πρὸς ἐπινοίᾳ καὶ φροντίδι τοῦ
μέλλοντος ὄντων, αὐτὸς ἄχρι τῆς ἑσπέρας ἔγραφε
συντάττων ἐπιτομὴν Πολυβίου.

V. Λέγεται δὲ καὶ Καῖσαρ οὐκ ἀμελεῖν τοῦ ἀνδρός,
ἀλλὰ καὶ προειπεῖν τοῖς ὑφ' ἑαυτὸν ἡγεμόσιν ἐν τῇ
μάχῃ μὴ κτείνειν Βροῦτον, ἀλλὰ φείδεσθαι, καὶ
παρασχόντα μὲν ἑκουσίως ἄγειν, εἰ δὲ ἀπομάχοιτο
πρὸς τὴν σύλληψιν, ἐᾶν καὶ μὴ βιάζεσθαι· καὶ ταῦτα
ποιεῖν τῇ μητρὶ τοῦ Βρούτου Σερβιλίᾳ χαριζόμενος.
2 ἐγνώκει γάρ, ὡς ἔοικε, νεανίας ὢν ἔτι τὴν Σερβιλίαν
ἐπιμανεῖσαν αὐτῷ, καὶ καθ' οὓς μάλιστα χρόνους ὁ
ἔρως ἐπέφλεγε γενόμενον τὸν Βροῦτον ἐπέπειστό πως
ἐξ ἑαυτοῦ γεγονέναι. . . .

VI. Γενομένης δὲ τῆς κατὰ Φάρσαλον ἥττης
καὶ Πομπηΐου μὲν ἐπὶ θάλασσαν διεκπεσόντος,
πολιορκουμένου δὲ τοῦ χάρακος, ἔλαθεν ὁ Βροῦτος
κατὰ πύλας πρὸς τόπον ἑλώδη καὶ μεστὸν ὑδάτων καὶ
καλάμου φερούσας ἐξελθὼν καὶ διὰ νυκτὸς ἀποσωθεὶς

rior. During the campaign, for whatever part of the day he was not with Pompey, he busied himself with books and literature, not only the rest of the time, but even before the great battle.[1] It was the height of summer, the heat was great (since they had encamped in marshy regions), and they that carried the tent of Brutus were slow in coming. But though he was thus all worn out, and though it was almost noon before he anointed himself and took a little food, nevertheless, while the rest were either sleeping or occupied with anxious thoughts about the future, he himself was busy until evening in making and writing out a compend of Polybius.

V. It is said, moreover, that Caesar also was concerned for his safety, and ordered his officers not to kill Brutus in the battle, but to spare him, and take him prisoner if he gave himself up voluntarily, and if he persisted in fighting against capture, to let him alone and do him no violence; and that Caesar did this out of regard for Servilia, the mother of Brutus. For while he was still a young man, as it seems, Caesar had been intimate with Servilia, who was madly in love with him, and he had some grounds for believing that Brutus, who was born at about the time when her passion was in full blaze, was his own son . . .

VI. After the defeat at Pharsalus, when Pompey had made his escape to the sea and his camp was besieged, Brutus went out unnoticed by a gate leading to a place that was marshy and full of water and reeds, and made his way

[1] At Pharsalus in Thessaly, in August of 48 B.C.

2 εἰς Λάρισσαν. ἐκεῖθεν δὲ γράψαντος αὐτοῦ Καῖσαρ
ἥσθη τε σωζομένῳ, καὶ κελεύσας πρὸς αὐτὸν ἐλθεῖν
οὐ μόνον ἀφῆκε τῆς αἰτίας, ἀλλὰ καὶ τιμώμενον ἐν

3 τοῖς μάλιστα περὶ αὑτὸν εἶχεν. οὐδενὸς δ' ὅπη φεύγοι
Πομπήϊος εἰπεῖν ἔχοντος, ἀλλ' ἀπορίας οὔσης, ὁδόν
τινα σὺν τῷ Βρούτῳ βαδίζων μόνος ἀπεπειρᾶτο τῆς

4 γνώμης. καὶ δόξαντος ἔκ τινων διαλογισμῶν ἄριστα
περὶ τῆς Πομπηΐου τεκμαίρεσθαι φυγῆς, ἀφεὶς τἆλλα

5 τὴν ἐπ' Αἰγύπτου συνέτεινεν. ἀλλὰ Πομπήϊον μέν,
ὥσπερ εἴκασε Βροῦτος, Αἰγύπτῳ προσβαλόντα τὸ
πεπρωμένον ἐδέξατο, Καίσαρα δὲ καὶ πρὸς Κάσσιον

6 ἐπράϋνε Βροῦτος. καὶ δὴ καὶ τῷ τῶν Λιβύων βασιλεῖ
προηγορῶν μὲν ἡττᾶτο τοῦ μεγέθους τῶν κατηγοριῶν,
δεόμενος δὲ καὶ παραιτούμενος περὶ τούτου πολλὴν

7 αὐτῷ διέσωσε τῆς ἀρχῆς. λέγεται δὲ Καῖσαρ, ὅτε
πρῶτον ἤκουσεν αὐτοῦ λέγοντος, εἰπεῖν πρὸς τοὺς
φίλους· "Οὗτος ὁ νεανίας οὐκ οἶδα μὲν ὃ βούλεται,

8 πᾶν δ' ὃ βούλεται σφόδρα βούλεται." τὸ γὰρ ἐμβριθὲς
αὐτοῦ καὶ μὴ ῥᾳδίως μηδὲ παντὸς ὑπήκοον τοῦ
δεομένου πρὸς χάριν, ἀλλ' ἐκ λογισμοῦ καὶ
προαιρέσεως τῶν καλῶν πρακτικόν, ὅποι τρέψειεν,

9 ἰσχυραῖς ἐχρῆτο ταῖς ὁρμαῖς καὶ τελεσιουργοῖς. πρὸς
δὲ τὰς ἀδίκους δεήσεις ἀκόλακευτος ἦν, καὶ τὴν ὑπὸ
τῶν ἀναισχύντως λιπαρούντων ἧτταν, ἣν ἔνιοι
δυσωπεῖσθαι καλοῦσιν, αἰσχίστην ἀνδρὶ μεγάλῳ
ποιούμενος εἰώθει λέγειν ὡς οἱ μηδὲν ἀρνεῖσθαι

safely by night to Larissa. From thence he wrote to Caesar, who was delighted at his safe escape, and bade him come to him, and not only pardoned him, but actually made him a highly honoured companion. Now, since no one could tell whither Pompey was fleeing, and all were in great perplexity, Caesar took a long walk with Brutus alone, and sounded him on the subject. Certain considerations advanced by Brutus made his opinion concerning Pompey's flight seem the best, and Caesar therefore renounced all other courses and hastened towards Egypt. But as for Pompey, he put in at Egypt, as Brutus conjectured, and there met his doom; as for Caesar, however, Brutus tried to soften him towards Cassius also. He also served as advocate for the king of Africa,[2] and though he lost the case, owing to the magnitude of the accusations against his client, still, by supplications and entreaties in his behalf he saved much of his kingdom for him. And it is said that Caesar, when he first heard Brutus speak in public, said to his friends: "I know not what this young man wants, but all that he wants he wants very much." For the weight of his character, and the fact that no one found it easy to make him listen to appeals for favour, but that he accomplished his ends by reasoning and the adoption of noble principles, made his efforts, whithersoever directed, powerful and efficacious. No flattery could induce him to grant an unjust petition, and that inability to withstand shameless importunity, which some call timidity, he regarded as most dis-

[2] Probably an error, either of Plutarch's, or of the MSS. In 47 B.C. Brutus pleaded unsuccessfully before Caesar the cause of Deiotarus, king of Galatia.

δυνάμενοι δοκοῦσιν αὐτῷ μὴ καλῶς τὴν ὥραν
διατεθεῖσθαι.

10   Μέλλων δὲ διαβαίνειν εἰς Λιβύην Καῖσαρ ἐπὶ
Κάτωνα καὶ Σκηπίωνα Βρούτῳ τὴν ἐντὸς Ἄλπεων
11 Γαλατίαν ἐπέτρεψεν εὐτυχίᾳ τινὶ τῆς ἐπαρχίας· τὰς
γὰρ ἄλλας ὕβρει καὶ πλεονεξίᾳ τῶν πεπιστευμένων
ὥσπερ αἰχμαλώτους διαφορούντων, ἐκείνοις καὶ τῶν
πρόσθεν ἀτυχημάτων παῦλα καὶ παραμυθία Βροῦτος
12 ἦν. καὶ τὴν χάριν εἰς Καίσαρα πάντων ἀνῆπτεν, ὡς
αὐτῷ μετὰ τὴν ἐπάνοδον περιϊόντι τὴν Ἰταλίαν
ἥδιστον θέαμα τὰς ὑπὸ Βρούτῳ πόλεις γενέσθαι, καὶ
Βροῦτον αὐτόν, αὔξοντα τὴν ἐκείνου τιμὴν καὶ
συνόντα κεχαρισμένως.

graceful in a great man, and he was wont to say that those who were unable to refuse anything, in his opinion, must have been corrupted in their youth.

When Caesar was about to cross over into Africa against Cato and Scipio, he put Brutus in charge of Cisalpine Gaul, to the great good-fortune of the province; for while the other provinces, owing to the insolence and rapacity of their governors, were plundered as though they had been conquered in war, to the people of his province Brutus meant relief and consolation even for their former misfortunes. And he attached the gratitude of all to Caesar, so that, after Caesar's return, and as he traversed Italy, he found the cities under Brutus a most pleasing sight, as well as Brutus himself, who enhanced his honour and was a delightful companion.

LUCIAN

Translation by M. D. Macleod

ΠΑΝΟΣ ΚΑΙ ΕΡΜΟΥ

ΠΑΝ

1. Χαῖρε, ὦ πάτερ Ἑρμῆ.

ΕΡΜΗΣ

Μὴ καὶ σύ γε. ἀλλὰ πῶς ἐγὼ σὸς πατήρ;

ΠΑΝ

Οὐχ ὁ Κυλλήνιος Ἑρμῆς ὢν τυγχάνεις;

ΕΡΜΗΣ

Καὶ μάλα. πῶς οὖν υἱὸς ἐμὸς εἶ;

ΠΑΝ

Μοιχίδιός εἰμι, ἐξ ἔρωτός σοι γενόμενος.

ΕΡΜΗΣ

Νὴ Δία, τράγου ἴσως τινὸς μοιχεύσαντος αἶγα·
ἐμοὶ γὰρ πῶς, κέρατα ἔχων καὶ ῥῖνα τοιαύτην καὶ

Dialogues of the Gods 2
Don't call me Daddy!

PAN AND HERMES

PAN
Good day to you, Hermes, Daddy mine.

HERMES
And a bad day to you. But how am I your daddy?

PAN
Aren't you Hermes of Cyllene?

HERMES
Yes. How, then, are you my son?

PAN
I'm your bastard boy, your love-child.

HERMES
Oh quite so, when some billy-goat, I suppose, led a nanny astray! How could you be mine, you with your horns and

πώγωνα λάσιον καὶ σκέλη διχαλὰ καὶ τραγικὰ καὶ
οὐρὰν ὑπὲρ τὰς πυγάς;

ΠΑΝ

Ὅσα ἂν ἀποσκώψῃς με, τὸν σεαυτοῦ υἱόν, ὦ
πάτερ, ἐπονείδιστον ἀποφαίνεις, μᾶλλον δὲ σεαυτόν,
ὃς τοιαῦτα γεννᾷς καὶ παιδοποιεῖς, ἐγὼ δὲ ἀναίτιος.

ΕΡΜΗΣ

Τίνα καὶ φῄς σου μητέρα; ἤ που ἔλαθον αἶγα
μοιχεύσας ἔγωγε;

ΠΑΝ

Οὐκ αἶγα ἐμοίχευσας, ἀλλ᾿ ἀνάμνησον σεαυτόν, εἴ
ποτε ἐν Ἀρκαδίᾳ παῖδα ἐλευθέραν ἐβιάσω. τί δακὼν
τὸν δάκτυλον ζητεῖς καὶ ἐπὶ πολὺ ἀπορεῖς; τὴν
Ἰκαρίου λέγω Πηνελόπην.

ΕΡΜΗΣ

270   Εἶτα τί παθοῦσα ἐκείνη ἀντ᾿ ἐμοῦ τράγῳ σε ὅμοιον
ἔτεκεν;

ΠΑΝ

2. Αὐτῆς ἐκείνης λόγον σοι ἐρῶ· ὅτε γάρ με
ἐξέπεμπεν ἐπὶ τὴν Ἀρκαδίαν, Ὦ παῖ, μήτηρ μέν σοι,
ἔφη, ἐγώ εἰμι, Πηνελόπη ἡ Σπαρτιᾶτις, τὸν πατέρα δὲ
γίνωσκε θεὸν ἔχων Ἑρμῆν Μαίας καὶ Διός. εἰ δὲ
κερασφόρος καὶ τραγοσκελὴς εἶ, μὴ λυπείτω σε·
ὁπότε γάρ μοι συνῄει ὁ πατὴρ ὁ σός, τράγῳ ἑαυτὸν

ugly snout and shaggy beard and a goat's cloven hooves and a tail over your behind?

PAN

When you jeer at me, daddy, you're mocking your own son, or rather yourself for producing such creatures as your children. It's not my fault.

HERMES

Who do you say your mother was? Perhaps I led a nanny astray without knowing it.

PAN

No, not a nanny. But try to remember if you ever forced your attentions on a freeborn girl in Arcadia. Why are you biting your nails and thinking so hard? Why so puzzled? I'm speaking of Icarius' girl, Penelope.[1]

HERMES

Then what possessed her to produce in you a child not like me but like a goat?

PAN

I'll tell you what she said herself. When she was packing me off to Arcadia, she said, "My boy, I, Penelope, a true blue Spartan, am your mother, but your father, let me tell you, is a god, Hermes, son of Maia and Zeus. Don't worry because you have horns and a goat's shanks, for when your father came courting me, he made himself into a goat so

---

[1] Lucian (with Cicero, *De Natura Deorum*, III, 22) follows Herodotus, II, 145 in making Pan the son of Penelope. There are other versions of his birth, of which the most important is the Homeric *Hymn to Pan* 34, where his mother is the daughter of Dryops.

ἀπείκασεν, ὡς λάθοι, καὶ διὰ τοῦτο ὅμοιος ἀπέβης τῷ τράγῳ.

Νὴ Δία, μέμνημαι ποιήσας τοιοῦτόν τι. ἐγὼ οὖν ὁ
271 ἐπὶ κάλλει μέγα φρονῶν, ἔτι ἀγένειος αὐτὸς ὢν σὸς πατὴρ κεκλήσομαι καὶ γέλωτα ὀφλήσω παρὰ πᾶσιν ἐπὶ τῇ εὐπαιδίᾳ;

3. Καὶ μὴν οὐ καταισχυνῶ σε, ὦ πάτερ· μουσικός τε γάρ εἰμι καὶ συρίζω πάνυ καπυρόν, καὶ ὁ Διόνυσος οὐδὲν ἐμοῦ ἄνευ ποιεῖν δύναται, ἀλλὰ ἑταῖρον καὶ θιασώτην πεποίηταί με, καὶ ἡγοῦμαι αὐτῷ τοῦ χοροῦ· καὶ τὰ ποίμνια δὲ εἰ θεάσαιό μου, ὁπόσα περὶ Τεγέαν καὶ ἀνὰ τὸ Παρθένιον ἔχω, πάνυ ἡσθήσῃ· ἄρχω δὲ καὶ τῆς Ἀρκαδίας ἁπάσης· πρῴην δὲ καὶ Ἀθηναίοις
272 συμμαχήσας οὕτως ἠρίστευσα Μαραθῶνι, ὥστε καὶ ἀριστεῖον ᾑρέθη μοι τὸ ὑπὸ τῇ ἀκροπόλει σπήλαιον. ἢν γοῦν εἰς Ἀθήνας ἔλθῃς, εἴσῃ ὅσον ἐκεῖ τοῦ Πανὸς ὄνομα.

4. Εἰπὲ δέ μοι, γεγάμηκας, ὦ Πάν, ἤδη; τοῦτο γάρ, οἶμαι, καλοῦσίν σε.

Οὐδαμῶς, ὦ πάτερ· ἐρωτικὸς γάρ εἰμι καὶ οὐκ ἂν ἀγαπήσαιμι συνὼν μιᾷ.

DIALOGUES OF THE GODS

that no one would notice him. That's why you've turned out like the goat."

HERMES

Ah, yes. I do remember doing something like that. Am I, then, to be called your father? I, who am so proud of my good looks! I, who've still got a smooth chin! Am I to be laughed at by all for having such a bonny boy?

PAN

But I won't disgrace you, father. I'm a musician and play the pipe loud and true. Dionysus is lost without me, and has made me his companion and fellow-reveller; I'm his dance-leader, and if you could see how many flocks I have around Tegea and on Parthenium, you'd be delighted. I'm lord and master of all Arcadia. Besides that, the other day, I fought so magnificently on the side of the Athenians at Marathon that a prize of valour was chosen for me—the cave under the Acropolis.[1] Anyhow, go to Athens and you'll soon find out what a great name Pan has there.

HERMES

Tell me, are you married yet, Pan? Pan's the name they give you, isn't it?

PAN

Of course not, daddy. I'm romantically inclined, and wouldn't like to have to confine my attentions to just one.

[1] Cf. Herodotus, VI, 105, Euripides, *Ion*, 492 ff., Lucian, *Double Indictment* 9, and *Lover of Lies* 3.

ΕΡΜΗΣ

Ταῖς οὖν αἰξὶ δηλαδὴ ἐπιχειρεῖς.

ΠΑΝ

Σὺ μὲν σκώπτεις, ἐγὼ δὲ τῇ τε Ἠχοῖ καὶ τῇ Πίτυϊ σύνειμι καὶ ἁπάσαις ταῖς τοῦ Διονύσου Μαινάσι καὶ πάνυ σπουδάζομαι πρὸς αὐτῶν.

ΕΡΜΗΣ

Οἶσθα οὖν, ὦ τέκνον, ὅ τι χαρίσῃ τὸ πρῶτον αἰτοῦντί μοι;

ΠΑΝ

Πρόσταττε, ὦ πάτερ· ἡμεῖς μὲν ἴδωμεν ταῦτα.

ΕΡΜΗΣ

Καὶ πρόσιθι μοι καὶ φιλοφρονοῦ· πατέρα δὲ ὅρα μὴ καλέσῃς με ἄλλου ἀκούοντος.

HERMES

No doubt, then, you try your luck with the nanny goats?

PAN

A fine jest coming from you! My lady-friends are Echo and Pitys and all the Maenads of Dionysus, and I'm in great demand with them.

HERMES

Please do me a favour, son. I've never asked one from you before.

PAN

Tell me what you want, daddy, and let me see to it.

HERMES

You may come here and pay your respects to me, but please don't call me daddy when anyone can hear.

PAUSANIAS

Translation by W. H. S. Jones

7   Κατὰ δὲ τὴν ἐς Ὀλυμπίαν ὁδόν, πρὶν ἢ δια-
βῆναι τὸν Ἀλφειόν, ἔστιν ὅρος ἐκ Σκιλλοῦντος
ἐρχομένῳ πέτραις ὑψηλαῖς ἀπότομον· ὀνομάζεται
δὲ Τυπαῖον τὸ ὅρος. κατὰ τούτου τὰς γυναῖκας
Ἠλείοις ἐστὶν ὠθεῖν νόμος, ἢν φωραθῶσιν ἐς τὸν
ἀγῶνα ἐλθοῦσαι τὸν Ὀλυμπικὸν ἢ καὶ ὅλως ἐν
ταῖς ἀπειρημέναις σφίσιν ἡμέραις διαβᾶσαι τὸν
Ἀλφειόν. οὐ μὴν οὐδὲ ἁλῶναι λέγουσιν οὐδεμίαν,
ὅτι μὴ Καλλιπάτειραν μόνην· εἰσὶ δὲ οἳ τὴν αὐτὴν
ταύτην Φερενίκην καὶ οὐ Καλλιπάτειραν καλοῦσιν.
8   αὕτη προαποφανόντος αὐτῇ τοῦ ἀνδρός, ἐξεικάσασα
αὐτὴν τὰ πάντα ἀνδρὶ γυμναστῇ, ἤγαγεν ἐς
Ὀλυμπίαν τὸν υἱὸν μαχούμενον· νικῶντος δὲ τοῦ
Πεισιρόδου, τὸ ἔρυμα ἐν ᾧ τοὺς γυμναστὰς ἔχουσιν
ἀπειλημμένους, τοῦτο ὑπερπηδῶσα ἡ Καλλιπάτειρα
ἐγυμνώθη. φωραθείσης δὲ ὅτι εἴη γυνή, ταύτην
ἀφιᾶσιν ἀζήμιον καὶ τῷ πατρὶ καὶ ἀδελφοῖς αὐτῆς καὶ

Description of Greece 5.6.7–8, 5.7.6–10

Tales of the Olympic games

As you go from Scillus along the road to Olympia, before you cross the Alpheius, there is a mountain with high, precipitous cliffs. It is called Mount Typaeum. It is a law of Elis to cast down it any women who are caught present at the Olympic games, or even on the other side of the Alpheius, on the days prohibited to women. However, they say that no woman has been caught, except Callipateira only; some, however, give the lady the name of Pherenice and not Callipateira. She, being a widow, disguised herself exactly like a gymnastic trainer, and brought her son to compete at Olympia. Peisirodus, for so her son was called, was victorious, and Callipateira, as she was jumping over the enclosure in which they keep the trainers shut up, bared her person. So her sex was discovered, but they let her go unpunished out of respect for her father, her broth-

τῷ παιδὶ αἰδῶ *νέμοντες*—ὑπῆρχον δὴ ἅπασιν αὐτοῖς
Ὀλυμπικαὶ νῖκαι—, ἐποίησαν δὲ *νόμον* ἐς τὸ ἔπειτα
ἐπὶ τοῖς γυμνασταῖς γυμνοὺς σφᾶς ἐς τὸν ἀγῶνα
ἐσέρχεσθαι. . . .

6   Ταῦτα μὲν δὴ ἔχει τρόπον τὸν εἰρημένον· ἐς δὲ τὸν
ἀγῶνα τὸν Ὀλυμπιακὸν λέγουσιν Ἠλείων οἱ τὰ
ἀρχαιότατα μνημονεύοντες Κρόνον τὴν ἐν οὐρανῷ
σχεῖν βασιλείαν πρῶτον καὶ ἐν Ὀλυμπίᾳ ποιηθῆναι
Κρόνῳ ναὸν ὑπὸ τῶν τότε ἀνθρώπων, οἳ ὠνομάζοντο
χρυσοῦν γένος· Διὸς δὲ τεχθέντος ἐπιτρέψαι Ῥέαν
τοῦ παιδὸς τὴν φρουρὰν τοῖς Ἰδαίοις Δακτύλοις,
καλουμένοις δὲ τοῖς αὐτοῖς τούτοις καὶ Κούρησιν·
ἀφικέσθαι δὲ αὐτοὺς ἐξ Ἴδης τῆς Κρητικῆς, Ἡρακλέα
καὶ Παιωναῖον καὶ Ἐπιμήδην καὶ Ἰάσιόν τε καὶ Ἴδαν·
7   τὸν δὲ Ἡρακλέα παίζοντα—εἶναι γὰρ δὴ αὐτὸν
πρεσβύτατον ἡλικίᾳ—συμβαλεῖν τοὺς ἀδελφοὺς ἐς
ἅμιλλαν δρόμου καὶ τὸν νικήσαντα ἐξ αὐτῶν κλάδῳ
στεφανῶσαι κοτίνου· παρεῖναι δὲ αὐτοῖς πολὺν δή τι
οὕτω τὸν κότινον ὡς τὰ χλωρὰ ἔτι τῶν φύλλων
ὑπεστρῶσθαι σφᾶς καθεύδοντας. κομισθῆναι δὲ ἐκ
τῆς Ὑπερβορέων γῆς τὸν κότινόν φασιν ὑπὸ τοῦ
Ἡρακλέους ἐς Ἕλληνας, εἶναι δὲ ἀνθρώπους οἳ ὑπὲρ
8   τὸν ἄνεμον οἰκοῦσι τὸν Βορέαν. πρῶτος μὲν ἐν ὕμνῳ
τῷ ἐς Ἀχαιίαν ἐποίησεν Ὠλὴν Λύκιος ἀφικέσθαι τὴν
Ἀχαιίαν ἐς Δῆλον ἐκ τῶν Ὑπερβορέων τούτων· ἔπειτα
δὲ ᾠδὴν Μελάνωπος Κυμαῖος ἐς Ὦπιν καὶ Ἑκαέργην
ᾖσεν, ὡς ἐκ τῶν Ὑπερβορέων καὶ αὗται πρότερον ἔτι
9   τῆς Ἀχαιίας ἀφίκοντο ἐς Δῆλον· Ἀριστέας δὲ ὁ

ers and her son, all of whom had been victorious at Olympia. But a law was passed that for the future trainers should strip before entering the arena. . . .

These things then are as I have described them. As for the Olympic games, the most learned antiquaries of Elis say that Cronus was the first king of heaven, and that in his honour a temple was built in Olympia by the men of that age, who were named the Golden Race. When Zeus was born, Rhea entrusted the guardianship of her son to the Dactyls of Ida, who are the same as those called Curetes. They came from Cretan Ida—Heracles, Paeonaeus, Epimedes, Iasius and Idas. Heracles, being the eldest, matched his brothers, as a game, in a running-race, and crowned the winner with a branch of wild olive, of which they had such a copious supply that they slept on heaps of its leaves while still green. It is said to have been introduced into Greece by Heracles from the land of the Hyperboreans, men living beyond the home of the North Wind. Olen the Lycian, in his hymn to Achaeia, was the first to say that from these Hyperboreans Achaeia came to Delos. Then Melanopus of Cyme composed an ode to Opis and Hecaërge, declaring that these, even before Achaeia, came to Delos from the Hyperboreans. And Aristeas of

Προκοννήσιος—μνήμην γὰρ ἐποιήσατο Ὑπερβορέων
καὶ οὗτος—τάχα τι καὶ πλέον περὶ αὐτῶν πεπυσμένος
ἂν εἴη παρὰ Ἰσσηδόνων, ἐς οὓς ἀφικέσθαι φησὶν ἐν
τοῖς ἔπεσιν. Ἡρακλεῖ οὖν πρόσεστι τῷ Ἰδαίῳ δόξα
τὸν τότε ἀγῶνα διαθεῖναι πρώτῳ καὶ Ὀλύμπια ὄνομα
θέσθαι· διὰ πέμπτου οὖν ἔτους αὐτὸν κατεστήσατο
ἄγεσθαι, ὅτι αὐτός τε καὶ οἱ ἀδελφοὶ πέντε ἦσαν
10 ἀριθμόν. Δία δὴ οἱ μὲν ἐνταῦθα παλαῖσαι καὶ αὐτῷ
Κρόνῳ περὶ τῆς ἀρχῆς, οἱ δὲ ἐπὶ κατειργασμένῳ
ἀγωνοθετῆσαί φασιν αὐτόν· νικῆσαι δὲ ἄλλοι τε
λέγονται καὶ ὅτι Ἀπόλλων παραδράμοι μὲν ἐρίζοντα
Ἑρμῆν, κρατῆσαι δὲ Ἄρεως πυγμῇ. τούτου δὲ
ἕνεκα καὶ τὸ αὔλημα Πυθικόν φασι τῷ πηδήματι
ἐπεισαχθῆναι τῶν πεντάθλων, ὡς τὸ μὲν ἱερὸν τοῦ
Ἀπόλλωνος τὸ αὔλημα ὄν, τὸν Ἀπόλλωνα δὲ
ἀνῃρημένον Ὀλυμπικὰς νίκας.

Proconnesus—for he too made mention of the Hyperboreans—may perhaps have learnt even more about them from the Issedones, to whom he says in his poem that he came. Heracles of Ida, therefore, has the reputation of being the first to have held, on the occasion I mentioned, the games, and to have called them Olympic. So he established the custom of holding them every fifth[1] year, because he and his brothers were five in number. Now some say that Zeus wrestled here with Cronus himself for the throne, while others say that he held the games in honour of his victory over Cronus. The record of victors include Apollo, who outran Hermes and beat Ares at boxing. It is for this reason, they say, that the Pythian flute-song is played while the competitors in the pentathlum are jumping; for the flute-song is sacred to Apollo, and Apollo won Olympic victories.

[1] That is, in Greek way of counting. Between two Olympic festivals there were only four complete intervening years, but the Greeks included both years in which consecutive festivals were held.

TERENCE

Translation by John Barsby

ACTUS I

I. I: MICIO.

MIC Storax! non rediit hac nocte a cena Aeschinus
neque servolorum quisquam qui advorsum ierant.
profecto hoc vere dicunt: si absis uspiam
aut ibi si cesses, evenire ea satius est
30   quae in te uxor dicit et quae in animo cogitat
irata quam illa quae parentes propitii.
uxor, si cesses, aut te amare cogitat
aut tete amari aut potare atque animo obsequi
et tibi bene esse soli, quom sibi sit male.
35   ego quia non rediit filius quae cogito et
quibus nunc sollicitor rebus! ne aut ille alserit
aut uspiam ceciderit aut praefregerit
aliquid. vah! quemquamne hominem in animo instituere
      aut
parare quod sit carius quam ipsest sibi!
40   atque ex me hic natus non est sed ex fratre. is adeo

The Brothers 26–77

Micio is lenient with his adoptive son Aeschines—much
to the disapproval of his disciplinarian brother

ACT ONE

Enter MICIO from his house.

MIC   (*calling down the street to a slave*) Storax! (*getting no re-
ply, to himself*) Aeschinus hasn't come back from that
dinner party last night, nor any of the slaves who went to
fetch him. It's quite true what they say: if you're out
somewhere and get home late, you're better off with
what an angry wife accuses you of or imagines than what
fond parents do. If you're late, your wife imagines that
you're in love or that someone has fallen in love with you
or else that you're drinking and enjoying yourself and
having fun on your own while she isn't. But in my case,
when my son hasn't returned, what dreadful things I
imagine, what anxieties I entertain! I only hope he hasn't
caught a cold or fallen somewhere or broken something.
Oh! Why does anybody want or acquire something that
will prove dearer to him than his own self? In fact, he's
not my own son by birth but my brother's. Now *he's* been

127

dissimili studiost iam inde ab adulescentia.
ego hanc clementem vitam urbanam atque otium
secutus sum et, quod fortunatum isti putant,
uxorem numquam habui. ille contra haec omnia.
45   ruri agere vitam, semper parce ac duriter
se habere. uxorem duxit, nati filii
duo. inde ego hunc maiorem adoptavi mihi,
eduxi e parvolo, habui, amavi pro meo.
in eo me oblecto, solum id est carum mihi.
50   ille ut item contra me habeat facio sedulo.
do, praetermitto, non necesse habeo omnia
pro meo iure agere. postremo, alii clanculum
patres quae faciunt, quae fert adulescentia,
ea ne me celet consuefeci filium.
55   nam qui mentiri aut fallere institerit patrem aut
audebit, tanto magis audebit ceteros.
pudore et liberalitate liberos
retinere satius esse credo quam metu.
haec fratri mecum non conveniunt neque placent.
60   venit ad me saepe clamitans "quid agis, Micio?
quor perdis adulescentem nobis? quor amat?
quor potat? quor tu his rebus sumptum suggeris,
vestitu nimio indulges? nimium ineptus es."
nimium ipsest durus praeter aequomque et bonum,
65   et errat longe mea quidem sententia
qui imperium credat gravius esse aut stabilius
vi quod fit quam illud quod amicitia adiungitur.
mea sic est ratio et sic animum induco meum:
malo coactus qui suom officium facit,
70   dum id rescitum iri credit, tantisper cavet;
si sperat fore clam, rursum ad ingenium redit.

a totally different character from me ever since we were young. I've pursued an easygoing life of leisure in the city, and I've never had a wife, which they reckon is a blessing. He's been exactly the opposite. He's lived in the country, choosing a life of thrift and hardship. He married and had two sons. Of these I adopted the elder one and have brought him up since he was a small child. I've treated him and loved him as my own. In him I find my pleasure; he's the only thing I really care about. And I do my best to see that he returns my affection. I'm generous, I turn a blind eye, I don't find it necessary to exert my authority all the time. In short I've accustomed my son not to hide from me those youthful escapades which others get up to behind their fathers' backs. A boy who sets out to lie and deceive his father and is bold enough to do that will be all the more bold with others. I believe that it is better to discipline children by gaining their respect and showing generosity than through fear. My brother doesn't agree with me on this; he just doesn't approve. He often comes to me shouting "What are you doing, Micio? Why are you ruining our boy? Why is he having a love affair? Why is he drinking? Why are you supplying him with money for these things? Why are you spoiling him with expensive clothes? You're being all too silly about it." Well, he's being all too strict, well beyond what is fair or right; and he's making a big mistake, in my opinion at least, if he thinks that authority imposed by force is stronger or surer than one based on affection. This is my philosophy and the principle I've adopted. A person who acts as he ought under threat of punishment watches his step only as long as he believes he'll be found out; if he thinks he can go undiscovered, he reverts to his natural

129

ill' quem beneficio adiungas ex animo facit,
studet par referre, praesens absensque idem erit.
hoc patriumst, potius consuefacere filium
75   sua sponte recte facere quam alieno metu:
hoc pater et dominus interest. hoc qui nequit,
fateatur nescire imperare liberis.

tendencies. A person who is won over by kindness acts from the heart. He is eager to repay you; he will be the same whether he is with you or not. A father's duty is to accustom his son to do right of his own accord rather than through fear of someone else. That's the difference between a father and a master. Anyone who can't see this should admit he has no idea how to manage children.

CICERO

Translation by Walter Miller

21   V. Detrahere igitur alteri aliquid et hominem hominis incommodo suum commodum augere magis est contra naturam quam mors, quam paupertas, quam dolor, quam cetera, quae possunt aut corpori accidere aut rebus externis. Nam principio tollit convictum humanum et societatem. Si enim sic erimus affecti, ut propter suum quisque emolumentum spoliet aut violet alterum, disrumpi necesse est, eam quae maxime est secundum naturam, humani generis

22   societatem. Ut, si unum quodque membrum sensum hunc haberet, ut posse putaret se valere, si proximi membri valetudinem ad se traduxisset, debilitari et interire totum corpus necesse esset, sic, si unus quisque nostrum ad se rapiat commoda aliorum detrahatque, quod cuique possit, emolumenti sui gratia, societas hominum et communitas evertatur necesse est. Nam sibi ut quisque malit, quod ad usum vitae pertineat, quam alteri acquirere, concessum

On Duties 3.5

Duty to one's neighbor

V. Well then, for a man to take something from his   21
neighbour and to profit by his neighbour's loss is more con-
trary to Nature than is death or poverty or pain or anything
else that can affect either our person or our property. For,
in the first place, injustice is fatal to social life and fellow-
ship between man and man. For, if we are so disposed that
each, to gain some personal profit, will defraud or injure
his neighbour, then those bonds of human society, which
are most in accord with Nature's laws, must of necessity be
broken. Suppose, by way of comparison, that each one of   22
our bodily members should conceive this idea and imagine
that it could be strong and well if it should draw off to itself
the health and strength of its neighbouring member, the
whole body would necessarily be enfeebled and die; so, if
each one of us should seize upon the property of his neigh-
bours and take from each whatever he could appropriate
to his own use, the bonds of human society must inevita-
bly be annihilated. For, without any conflict with Nature's
laws, it is granted that everybody may prefer to secure
for himself rather than for his neighbour what is essential

est non repugnante natura, illud natura non patitur, ut alio-
rum spoliis nostras facultates, copias, opes augeamus.

23   Neque vero hoc solum natura, id est iure gentium, sed
etiam legibus populorum, quibus in singulis civitatibus res
publica continetur, eodem modo constitutum est, ut non
liceat sui commodi causa nocere alteri; hoc enim spectant
leges, hoc volunt, incolumem esse civium coniunctionem;
quam qui dirimunt, eos morte, exsilio, vinclis, damno coër-
cent.

    Atque hoc multo magis efficit ipsa naturae ratio, quae
est lex divina et humana; cui parere qui velit (omnes autem
parebunt, qui secundum naturam volent vivere), num-
quam committet, ut alienum appetat et id, quod alteri de-
24 traxerit, sibi adsumat. Etenim multo magis est secundum
naturam excelsitas animi et magnitudo itemque comitas,
iustitia, liberalitas quam voluptas, quam vita, quam di-
vitiae; quae quidem contemnere et pro nihilo ducere com-
parantem cum utilitate communi magni animi et excelsi
est. [Detrahere autem de altero sui commodi causa magis
est contra naturam quam mors, quam dolor, quam cetera
generis eiusdem.]

25   Itemque magis est secundum naturam pro omnibus
gentibus, si fieri possit, conservandis aut iuvandis maximos
labores molestiasque suscipere imitantem Herculem il-
lum, quem hominum fama beneficiorum memor in conci-
lio caelestium collocavit, quam vivere in solitudine non

for the conduct of life; but Nature's laws do forbid us to increase our means, wealth, and resources by despoiling others.

But this principle is established not by Nature's laws   23
alone (that is, by the common rules of equity), but also by the statutes of particular communities, in accordance with which in individual states the public interests are maintained. In all these it is with one accord ordained that no man shall be allowed for the sake of his own advantage to injure his neighbour. For it is to this that the laws have regard; this is their intent, that the bonds of union between citizens should not be impaired; and any attempt to destroy these bonds is repressed by the penalty of death, exile, imprisonment, or fine.

Again, this principle follows much more effectually directly from the Reason which is in Nature, which is the law of gods and men. If anyone will hearken to that voice (and all will hearken to it who wish to live in accord with Nature's laws), he will never be guilty of coveting anything that is his neighbour's or of appropriating to himself what he has taken from his neighbour. Then, too, loftiness and   24
greatness of spirit, and courtesy, justice, and generosity are much more in harmony with Nature than are selfish pleasure, riches, and life itself; but it requires a great and lofty spirit to despise these latter and count them as naught, when one weighs them over against the common weal. [But for anyone to rob his neighbour for his own profit is more contrary to Nature than death, pain, and the like.]

In like manner it is more in accord with Nature to emu-   25
late the great Hercules and undergo the greatest toil and trouble for the sake of aiding or saving the world, if possible, than to live in seclusion, not only free from all care, but

modo sine ullis molestiis, sed etiam in maximis voluptatibus abundantem omnibus copiis, ut excellas etiam pulchritudine et viribus.

Quocirca optimo quisque et splendidissimo ingenio longe illam vitam huic anteponit. Ex quo efficitur hominem naturae oboedientem homini nocere non posse.

26   Deinde, qui alterum violat, ut ipse aliquid commodi consequatur, aut nihil existimat se facere contra naturam aut magis fugiendam censet mortem, paupertatem, dolorem, amissionem etiam liberorum, propinquorum, amicorum quam facere cuiquam iniuriam. Si nihil existimat contra naturam fieri hominibus violandis, quid cum eo disseras, qui omnino hominem ex homine tollat? sin fugiendum id quidem censet, sed multo illa peiora, mortem, paupertatem, dolorem, errat in eo, quod ullum aut corporis aut fortunae vitium vitiis animi gravius existimat.

revelling in pleasures and abounding in wealth, while excelling others also in beauty and strength. Thus Hercules denied himself and underwent toil and tribulation for the world, and, out of gratitude for his services, popular belief has given him a place in the council of the gods.

The better and more noble, therefore, the character with which a man is endowed, the more does he prefer the life of service to the life of pleasure. Whence it follows that man, if he is obedient to Nature, cannot do harm to his fellow-man.

Finally, if a man wrongs his neighbour to gain some advantage for himself, he must either imagine that he is not acting in defiance of Nature or he must believe that death, poverty, pain, or even the loss of children, kinsmen, or friends, is more to be shunned than an act of injustice against another. If he thinks he is not violating the laws of Nature, when he wrongs his fellow-men, how is one to argue with the individual who takes away from man all that makes him man? But if he believes that, while such a course should be avoided, the other alternatives are much worse—namely, death, poverty, pain—he is mistaken in thinking that any ills affecting either his person or his property are more serious than those affecting his soul. 26

CAESAR

Translation by H. J. Edwards

17   Caesar his de causis quas commemoravi Rhenum transire decreverat; sed navibus transire neque satis tutum esse arbitrabatur, neque suae neque populi Romani dignitatis esse statuebat. Itaque, etsi summa difficultas faciendi pontis proponebatur propter latitudinem, rapiditatem altitudinemque fluminis, tamen id sibi contendendum aut aliter non traducendum exercitum existimabat. Rationem pontis hanc instituit. Tigna bina sesquipedalia paulum ab imo praeacuta dimensa ad altitudinem fluminis intervallo pedum duorum inter se iungebat. Haec cum machinationibus immissa in flumen defixerat fistucisque adegerat, non sublicae modo directe ad perpendiculum, sed prone ac fastigate, ut secundum naturam fluminis procumberent, his item contraria duo ad eundem modum iuncta intervallo pedum quadragenum ab inferiore parte contra vim atque impetum fluminis conversa statuebat. Haec

Gallic War 4.17–19

The bridge on the river Rhine

For the reasons above mentioned Caesar had decided
to cross the Rhine; but he deemed it scarcely safe, and
ruled it unworthy of his own and the Romans' dignity, to
cross in boats. And so, although he was confronted with the
greatest difficulty in making a bridge, by reason of the
breadth, the rapidity, and the depth of the river, he still
thought that he must make that effort, or else not take his
army across. He proceeded to construct a bridge on the
following plan. He caused pairs of balks eighteen inches
thick, sharpened a little way from the base and measured
to suit the depth of the river, to be coupled together at an
interval of two feet. These he lowered into the river by
means of rafts, and set fast, and drove home by rammers;
not, like piles, straight up and down, but leaning forward at
a uniform slope, so that they inclined in the direction of the
stream. Opposite to these, again, were planted two balks
coupled in the same fashion, at a distance of forty feet from
base to base of each pair, slanted against the force and on-

utraque insuper bipedalibus trabibus immissis, quantum
eorum tignorum iunctura distabat, binis utrimque fibulis
ab extrema parte distinebantur; quibus disclusis atque in
contrariam partem revinctis tanta erat operis firmitudo
atque ea rerum natura, ut, quo maior vis aquae se incitavis-
set, hoc artius illigata tenerentur. Haec derecta materia
iniecta contexebantur ac longuriis cratibusque consterne-
bantur; ac nihilo setius sublicae et ad inferiorem partem
fluminis oblique agebantur, quae pro ariete subiectae et
cum omni opere coniunctae vim fluminis exciperent, et
aliae item supra pontem mediocri spatio, ut, si arborum
trunci sive naves deiciendi operis essent a barbaris missae,
his defensoribus earum rerum vis minueretur neu ponti
nocerent.

18   Diebus decem, quibus materia coepta erat comportari,
omni opere effecto exercitus traducitur. Caesar ad utram-
que partem pontis firmo praesidio relicto in fines Sugam-
brorum contendit. Interim a compluribus civitatibus ad
eum legati veniunt; quibus pacem atque amicitiam peten-
tibus liberaliter respondit obsidesque ad se adduci iubet.
Sugambri ex eo tempore quo pons institui coeptus est fuga

rush of the stream.[1] These pairs of balks had two-foot transoms let into them atop, filling the interval at which they were coupled, and were kept apart by a pair of braces on the outer side at each end. So, as they were held apart and contrariwise clamped together, the stability of the structure was so great and its character such that, the greater the force and thrust of the water, the tighter were the balks held in lock. These trestles[2] were interconnected by timber laid over at right angles, and floored with long poles and wattlework. And further, piles were driven in aslant on the side facing down stream, thrust out below like a buttress and close joined with the whole structure, so as to take the force of the stream; and others likewise at a little distance above the bridge, so that if trunks of trees, or vessels, were launched by the natives to break down the structure, these fenders might lessen the force of such shocks, and prevent them from damaging the bridge.

The whole work was completed in ten days from that on which the collecting of timber began, and the army was taken across. Leaving a strong post at either end of the bridge, Caesar pressed on into the territory of the Sugambri. Meanwhile from several states deputies came to him, to whose request for peace and friendship he replied in generous fashion, and ordered hostages to be brought to him. But from the moment when the bridge be-

---

[1] That is to say, the actual roadway of the bridge was narrower than forty feet by the inward slant of each pair of balks. Or *ab inferiore parte* may mean "on the side down stream."

[2] *i.e.* each set of balks and transoms.

comparata, hortantibus eis quos ex Tencteris atque Usipe-
tibus apud se habebant, finibus suis excesserant suaque
omnia exportaverant seque in solitudinem ac silvas abdi-
derant.

19   Caesar paucos dies in eorum finibus moratus omni-
bus vicis aedificiisque incensis frumentisque succisis se in
fines Ubiorum recepit atque eis auxilium suum pollicitus,
si ab Suebis premerentur, haec ab eis cognovit: Suebos,
posteaquam per exploratores pontem fieri comperissent,
more suo concilio habito nuntios in omnes partes dimi-
sisse, uti de oppidis demigrarent, liberos, uxores suaque
omnia in silvis deponerent, atque omnes qui arma ferre
possent unum in locum convenirent: hunc esse delectum
medium fere regionum earum, quas Suebi obtinerent: hic
Romanorum adventum exspectare atque ibi decertare
constituisse. Quod ubi Caesar comperit, omnibus rebus eis
confectis, quarum rerum causa traducere exercitum con-
stituerat, ut Germanis metum iniceret, ut Sugambros ul-
cisceretur, ut Ubios obsidione liberaret, diebus omnino
decem et octo trans Rhenum consumptis satis et ad lau-
dem et ad utilitatem profectum arbitratus se in Galliam
recepit pontemque rescidit.

gan to be constructed the Sugambri, at the instigation of the Tencteri and Usipetes among them, had been preparing for flight; and now they had evacuated their territory, carried off all their stuff, and hidden themselves in the remote part of the forests.

Caesar tarried for a few days in their territory, until he had burnt all the villages and buildings, and cut down the corn-crops. Then he withdrew into the territory of the Ubii; and, after a promise of his help to them, if they were hard pressed by the Suebi, he received the following information from them. The Suebi, when they had discovered by means of their scouts that a bridge was being built, held a convention according to their custom, and despatched messengers to all quarters, ordering the people to remove from their towns, to lodge their children and all their stuff in the woods, and to assemble in one place all men capable of bearing arms. The place chosen was about the middle of the districts occupied by the Suebi; here they were awaiting the approach of the Romans, having determined to fight the decisive battle on this spot. By the time when Caesar learnt this he had accomplished all the objects for which he had determined to lead his army across the Rhine—to strike terror into the Germans, to take vengeance on the Sugambri, to deliver the Ubii from a state of blockade. So, having spent in all eighteen days across the Rhine, and advanced far enough, as he thought, to satisfy both honour and expediency, he withdrew into Gaul and broke up the bridge.

LUCRETIUS

Translation by W. H. D. Rouse;
revised by Martin F. Smith

Suave, mari magno turbantibus aequora ventis,
e terra magnum alterius spectare laborem;
non quia vexari quemquamst iucunda voluptas,
sed quibus ipse malis careas quia cernere suave est.
5   suave etiam belli certamina magna tueri
per campos instructa tua sine parte pericli.
sed nil dulcius est bene quam munita tenere
edita doctrina sapientum templa serena,
despicere unde queas alios passimque videre
10 errare atque viam palantis quaerere vitae,
certare ingenio, contendere nobilitate,
noctes atque dies niti praestante labore
ad summas emergere opes rerumque potiri.
o miseras hominum mentes, o pectora caeca!
15 qualibus in tenebris vitae quantisque periclis
degitur hoc aevi quodcumquest! nonne videre
nil aliud sibi naturam latrare, nisi utqui
corpore seiunctus dolor absit, mensque fruatur
iucundo sensu cura semota metuque?

On the Nature of Things 2.1–61
The Epicurean ideal: peace of mind

Pleasant it is, when on the great sea the winds trouble the waters, to gaze from shore upon another's great tribulation: not because any man's troubles are a delectable joy, but because to perceive what ills you are free from yourself is pleasant. Pleasant is it also to behold great encounters of warfare arrayed over the plains, with no part of yours in the peril. But nothing is more delightful than to possess lofty sanctuaries serene, well fortified by the teachings of the wise, whence you may look down upon others and behold them all astray, wandering abroad and seeking the path of life:—the strife of wits, the fight for precedence, all labouring night and day with surpassing toil to mount upon the pinnacle of riches and to lay hold on power. O pitiable minds of men, O blind intelligences! In what gloom of life, in how great perils is passed all your poor span of time ! not to see that all nature barks for is this, that pain be removed away out of the body, and that the mind, kept away from care and fear, enjoy a feeling of delight!

20   Ergo corpoream ad naturam pauca videmus
     esse opus omnino, quae demant cumque dolorem,
     delicias quoque uti multas substernere possint;
     gratius interdum neque natura ipsa requirit,
     si non aurea sunt iuvenum simulacra per aedes
25   lampadas igniferas manibus retinentia dextris,
     lumina nocturnis epulis ut suppeditentur,
     nec domus argento fulget auroque renidet
     nec citharae reboant laqueata aurataque templa,
     cum tamen inter se prostrati in gramine molli
30   propter aquae rivum sub ramis arboris altae
     non magnis opibus iucunde corpora curant,
     praesertim cum tempestas adridet et anni
     tempora conspergunt viridantis floribus herbas.
     nec calidae citius decedunt corpore febres,
35   textilibus si in picturis ostroque rubenti
     iacteris, quam si in plebeia veste cubandum est.

     Quapropter quoniam nil nostro in corpore gazae
     proficiunt neque nobilitas nec gloria regni,
     quod superest, animo quoque nil prodesse putandum;
40   si non forte, tuas legiones per loca campi
     fervere cum videas belli simulacra cientis,
     subsidiis magnis et equum vi constabilitas,
     ornatas armis pariter pariterque animatas,

---

[1] According to Epicurus, pleasure is limited, and the limit of pleasure for the body is reached when the natural and necessary desires are satisfied and the pain caused by want is removed.

[2] 24–26 are in imitation of Homer, *Od.* 7.100–102.

Therefore we see that few things altogether are necessary for the bodily nature, only such in each case as take pain away,[1] and can also spread for our use many delights; nor does nature herself ever crave anything more pleasurable, if there be no golden images of youths about the house, upholding fiery torches in their right hands that light may be provided for nightly revellings,[2] if the hall does not shine with silver and glitter with gold, if no crossbeams panelled and gilded echo the lyre, when all the same[3] stretched forth in groups upon the soft grass beside a rill of water under the branches of a tall tree men merrily refresh themselves at no great cost, especially when the weather smiles, and the season of the year besprinkles the green herbage with flowers. And no quicker do hot fevers fly away from your body, if you have pictured tapestry and blushing purple to toss upon, than if you must lie sick under the poor man's blanket.

Therefore, since treasures profit nothing for our body, nor noble birth nor the glory of royalty, we must further think that for the mind also they are unprofitable; unless by any chance, when you behold your legions seething over the spacious Plain[4] as they evoke war in mimicry, established firm with mighty supports and a mass of cavalry, marshalled all in arms cap-à-pie and all full of one spirit,

[3] That is, despite the lack of the luxuries listed in 24–28. The desire for such luxuries is neither natural nor necessary, and therefore must be banished.

[4] *Campi* (40) probably refers to the Campus Martius at Rome.

147

LUCRETIUS

his tibi tum rebus timefactae religiones
45 effugiunt animo pavidae, mortisque timores
tum vacuum pectus linquunt curaque solutum.
quod si ridicula haec ludibriaque esse videmus,
re veraque metus hominum curaeque sequaces
nec metuunt sonitus armorum nec fera tela
50 audacterque inter reges rerumque potentis
versantur neque fulgorem reverentur ab auro
nec clarum vestis splendorem purpureai,
quid dubitas quin omni' sit haec rationi' potestas,
omnis cum in tenebris praesertim vita laboret?
55 nam veluti pueri trepidant atque omnia caecis
in tenebris metuunt, sic nos in luce timemus
interdum nilo quae sunt metuenda magis quam
quae pueri in tenebris pavitant finguntque futura.
hunc igitur terrorem animi tenebrasque necessest
60 non radii solis neque lucida tela diei
discutiant, sed naturae species ratioque.

then these things scare your superstitious fears and drive them in panic flight from your mind, and death's terrors then leave your heart unpossessed and free from care. But if we see these things to be ridiculous and a mere mockery, if in truth men's fears and haunting cares fear neither the clang of arms nor wild weapons, if they boldly mingle with kings and sovereigns of the world, if they respect not the sheen of gold nor the glowing light of crimson raiment, why doubt you that this power wholly belongs to reason, especially since life is one long struggle in the dark? For just as children tremble and fear all things in blind darkness, so we in the light fear, at times, things that are no more to be feared than what children shiver at in the dark and imagine to be at hand. This terror of the mind, therefore, and this gloom must be dispelled, not by the sun's rays nor the bright shafts of day, but by the aspect and law of nature.

VIRGIL

Translation by H. Rushton Fairclough;
revised by G. P. Goold

Conticuere omnes intentique ora tenebant.
inde toro pater Aeneas sic orsus ab alto:
    "Infandum, regina, iubes renovare dolorem,
Troianas ut opes et lamentabile regnum
5   eruerint Danai, quaeque ipse miserrima vidi
et quorum pars magna fui. quis talia fando
Myrmidonum Dolopumve aut duri miles Ulixi
temperet a lacrimis? et iam nox umida caelo
praecipitat suadentque cadentia sidera somnos.
10 sed si tantus amor casus cognoscere nostros
et breviter Troiae supremum audire laborem,
quamquam animus meminisse horret luctuque refugit,
incipiam.
      "Fracti bello fatisque repulsi
ductores Danaum, tot iam labentibus annis,
15 instar montis equum divina Palladis arte
aedificant sectaque intexunt abiete costas;
votum pro reditu simulant; ea fama vagatur.
huc delecta virum sortiti corpora furtim
includunt caeco lateri penitusque cavernas

150

Aeneid 2.1–56

Aeneas begins to tell Dido about the fall of Troy

All were hushed, and kept their rapt gaze upon him; then from his raised couch father Aeneas thus began:

"Too deep for words, O queen, is the grief you bid me renew, how the Greeks overthrew Troy's wealth and woeful realm—the sights most piteous that I saw myself and wherein I played no small role. What Myrmidon or Dolopian, or soldier of the stern Ulysses, could refrain from tears in telling such a tale? And now dewy night is speeding from the sky and the setting stars counsel sleep. Yet if such is your desire to learn of our disasters, and in few words to hear of Troy's last agony, though my mind shudders to remember and has recoiled in pain, I will begin.

"Broken in war and thwarted by the fates, the Danaan chiefs, now that so many years were gliding by, build by Pallas' divine art a horse of mountainous bulk, and interweave its ribs with planks of fir. They pretend it is an offering for their safe return; this is the rumour that goes abroad. Here, within its dark sides, they stealthily enclose the choicest of their stalwart men and deep within they fill

20   ingentis uterumque armato milite complent.
       "Est in conspectu Tenedos, notissima fama
    insula, dives opum, Priami dum regna manebant,
    nunc tantum sinus et statio male fida carinis:
    huc se provecti deserto in litore condunt.
25   nos abiisse rati et vento petiisse Mycenas.
    ergo omnis longo solvit se Teucria luctu.
    panduntur portae; iuvat ire et Dorica castra
    desertosque videre locos litusque relictum.
    hic Dolopum manus, hic saevus tendebat Achilles,
30   classibus hic locus, hic acie certare solebant.
    pars stupet innuptae donum exitiale Minervae
    et molem mirantur equi; primusque Thymoetes
    duci intra muros hortatur et arce locari,
    sive dolo seu iam Troiae sic fata ferebant.
35   at Capys, et quorum melior sententia menti,
    aut pelago Danaum insidias suspectaque dona
    praecipitare iubent subiectisque urere flammis,
    aut terebrare cavas uteri et temptare latebras.
    scinditur incertum studia in contraria vulgus.
40   "Primus ibi ante omnis, magna comitante caterva,
    Laocoon ardens summa decurrit ab arce
    et procul: 'o miseri, quae tanta insania, cives?
    creditis avectos hostis? aut ulla putatis
    dona carere dolis Danaum? sic notus Ulixes?
45   aut hoc inclusi ligno occultantur Achivi,
    aut haec in nostros fabricata est machina muros,
    inspectura domos venturaque desuper urbi,
    aut aliquis latet error; equo ne credite, Teucri.
    quidquid id est, timeo Danaos et dona ferentis.'

the huge cavern of the belly with armed soldiery.

"There lies in sight an island well known to fame, Tenedos, rich in wealth while Priam's kingdom stood, now but a bay and an unsafe anchorage for ships. Hither they sail and hide themselves on the barren shore. We thought they had gone and before the wind were bound for Mycenae. So all the Teucrian land frees itself from its long sorrow. The gates are opened; it is a joy to go and see the Doric camp, the deserted stations and forsaken shore. Here the Dolopian bands encamped, here cruel Achilles; here lay the fleet; here they used to meet us in battle. Some are amazed at maiden Minerva's gift of death, and marvel at the massive horse: and first Thymoetes urges that it be drawn within our walls and lodged in the citadel; either it was treachery or the doom of Troy was already tending that way. But Capys, and they whose minds were wiser in counsel, bid us either hurl headlong into the sea this guile of the Greeks, this distrusted gift, or fire it with flames heaped beneath; or else pierce and probe the hollow hiding place of the belly. The wavering crowd is torn into opposing factions.

"Then, foremost of all and with a great throng following, Laocoön in hot haste runs down from the citadel's height, and cries from afar: 'My poor countrymen, what monstrous madness is this? Do you believe the foe has sailed away? Do you think that any gifts of the Greeks are free from treachery? Is Ulysses known to be this sort of man? Either enclosed in this frame there lurk Achaeans, or this has been built as an engine of war against our walls, to spy into our homes and come down upon the city from above; or some trickery lurks inside. Men of Troy, trust not the horse. Whatever it be, I fear the Greeks, even when

50   sic fatus validis ingentem viribus hastam
       in latus inque feri curvam compagibus alvum
       contorsit. stetit illa tremens, uteroque recusso
       insonuere cavae gemitumque dedere cavernae.
       et si fata deum, si mens non laeva fuisset,
55   impulerat ferro Argolicas foedare latebras,
       Troiaque nunc staret, Priamique arx alta, maneres.

bringing gifts.' So saying, with mighty force he hurled his great spear at the beast's side and the arched frame of the belly. The spear stood quivering and with the cavity's reverberation the vaults rang hollow, sending forth a moan. And had the gods' decrees, had our mind not been perverse, he would have driven us to violate with steel the Argive den, and Troy would now be standing, and you, lofty citadel of Priam, would still abide!

HORACE

Translation by Niall Rudd

18

Nullam, Vare, sacra vite prius severis arborem
circa mite solum Tiburis et moenia Catili.
siccis omnia nam dura deus proposuit, neque
mordaces aliter diffugiunt sollicitudines.
5   quis post vina gravem militiam aut pauperiem crepat?
quis non te potius, Bacche pater, teque, decens Venus?
ac ne quis modici transiliat munera Liberi,
Centaurea monet cum Lapithis rixa super mero ·
debellata, monet Sithoniis non levis Euhius,
10   cum fas atque nefas exiguo fine libidinum
discernunt avidi. non ego te, candide Bassareu,

---

[1] A founder of Tibur.

[2] A name of Bacchus, from the Bacchanals' cry of "Euhoe!"

[3] Another name for Bacchus, connected with Bassaris, a Thracian Maenad. ·

Odes 1.18, 1.37

18

The blessings and dangers of wine

Varus, you should plant no tree in preference to the god-given vine around the genial soil of Tibur and the walls of Catilus;[1] for the gods have ordained that everything should be hard for the abstemious, and there is no other way to dispel the worries that gnaw the heart. After wine, who rattles on about the hardships of war or poverty? Who does not rather talk of you, Bacchus, and you, lovely Venus?

Yet no one must abuse by excess the gifts of the moderate God of Freedom. That is the lesson of the drunken brawl over unmixed wine between the Centaurs and Lapiths that ended in a battle. That is the lesson of Euhius[2] who came down heavily on the Sithonians when, in their eagerness for sex, they drew too fine a line between right and wrong. As for me, I shall never shake you, fair Bassareus,[3] against your will, nor shall I rudely expose to

invitum quatiam, nec variis obsita frondibus
sub divum rapiam. saeva tene cum Berecyntio
cornu tympana, quae subsequitur caecus Amor sui
15   et tollens vacuum plus nimio Gloria verticem
arcanique Fides prodiga, perlucidior vitro.

37

Nunc est bibendum, nunc pede libero
pulsanda tellus, nunc Saliaribus
    ornare pulvinar deorum
       tempus erat dapibus, sodales,
5   antehac nefas depromere Caecubum
cellis avitis, dum Capitolio
    regina dementis ruinas
       funus et imperio parabat
contaminato cum grege turpium
10   morbo virorum, quidlibet impotens
    sperare fortunaque dulci
       ebria. sed minuit furorem
vix una sospes navis ab ignibus,
mentemque lymphatam Mareotico

the daylight things that are hidden under multicoloured leaves.[4] Silence the wild tambourines and the Berecyntian pipe; they are attended by blind Self-love, and Glory that holds her empty head far too high, and Trust of the sort that lavishly gives away secrets and is more utterly transparent than glass.

37

The fall of Cleopatra

Now let the drinking begin! Now let us thump the ground with unfettered feet! Now is the time, my friends, to load the couches of the gods with a feast fit for the Salii![5]

Before this[6] it was sacrilege to bring the Caecuban out from our fathers' cellars, at a time when the queen, along with her troop of disgustingly perverted men, was devising mad ruin for the Capitol and death for the empire—a woman so out of control that she could hope for anything at all, drunk, as she was, with the sweet wine of success.

But her frenzy was sobered by the survival of scarcely one ship from the flames; and her mind, crazed with

[4] The god's mystic emblems were displayed on solemn occasions; for the rest they were covered with leaves of ivy, pine, and vine, and kept in a chest.

[5] The dance of gratitude to Mars leads naturally to the Salii, who were his priests. They performed a strenuous dance, and like other priests had lavish banquets.

[6] Before the suicide of Cleopatra in Alexandria in 30 B.C., following her defeat at Actium in the previous year.

15   redegit in veros timores
             Caesar ab Italia volantem
remis adurgens, accipiter velut
mollis columbas aut leporem citus
      venator in campis nivalis
20   Haemoniae, daret ut catenis
fatale monstrum; quae generosius
perire quaerens nec muliebriter
      expavit ensem nec latentis
             classe cita reparavit oras;
25 ausa et iacentem visere regiam
vultu sereno, fortis et asperas
      tractare serpentis, ut atrum
             corpore combiberet venenum,
deliberata morte ferocior,
30 saevis Liburnis scilicet invidens
      privata deduci superbo
             non humilis mulier triumpho.

Mareotic wine,[7] was brought down to face real terror when Caesar pursued her as she flew away from Italy with oars, like a hawk after a gentle dove or a speedy hunter after a hare on the snowy plains of Thessaly, to put that monster of doom safely in chains.

Determined to die more nobly, she showed no womanly fear of the sword, nor did she use her swift fleet to gain some hidden shore. She had the strength of mind to gaze on her ruined palace with a calm countenance, and the courage to handle the sharp-toothed serpents, letting her body drink in their black venom. Once she had resolved to die she was all the more defiant—determined, no doubt, to cheat the cruel Liburnians: she would not be stripped of her royalty and conveyed to face a jeering triumph: no humble woman she.

[7] From the region of Lake Mareotis, about 20 miles south of Memphis and 25 miles west of the Nile.

LIVY

Translation by B. O. Foster

IX. Iam res Romana adeo erat valida ut cuilibet finiti-
marum civitatum bello par esset; sed penuria mulierum
hominis aetatem duratura magnitudo erat, quippe quibus
2 nec domi spes prolis nec cum finitimis conubia essent.
Tum ex consilio patrum Romulus legatos circa vicinas gen-
tes misit, qui societatem conubiumque novo populo pete-
3 rent: urbes quoque, ut cetera, ex infimo nasci; dein, quas
sua virtus ac di iuvent, magnas opes sibi magnumque no-
4 men facere; satis scire origini Romanae et deos adfuisse et
non defuturam virtutem; proinde ne gravarentur homines
5 cum hominibus sanguinem ac genus miscere. Nusquam
benigne legatio audita est; adeo simul spernebant, simul
tantam in medio crescentem molem sibi ac posteris suis

History of Rome 1.9

The rape of the Sabine women

IX. Rome was now strong enough to hold her own in
war with any of the adjacent states; but owing to the want
of women a single generation was likely to see the end of
her greatness, since she had neither prospect of posterity
at home nor the right of intermarriage with her neigh-
bours. So, on the advice of the senate, Romulus sent en-
voys round among all the neighbouring nations to solicit
for the new people an alliance and the privilege of inter-
marrying. Cities, they argued, as well as all other things,
take their rise from the lowliest beginnings. As time goes
on, those which are aided by their own worth and by the fa-
vour of Heaven achieve great power and renown. They
said they were well assured that Rome's origin had been
blessed with the favour of Heaven, and that worth would
not be lacking; their neighbours should not be reluctant to
mingle their stock and their blood with the Romans, who
were as truly men as they were. Nowhere did the embassy
obtain a friendly hearing. In fact men spurned, at the same
time that they feared, both for themselves and their de-
scendants, that great power which was then growing up in

metuebant. A plerisque rogitantibus dimissi, ecquod fe-
minis quoque asylum aperuissent; id enim demum conpar
6 conubium fore. Aegre id Romana pubes passa, et haud
dubie ad vim spectare res coepit. Cui tempus locumque
aptum ut daret Romulus, aegritudinem animi dissimulans
ludos ex industria parat Neptuno equestri sollemnis; Con-
7 sualia vocat. Indici deinde finitimis spectaculum iubet,
quantoque apparatu tum sciebant aut poterant, concele-
8 brant, ut rem claram exspectatamque facerent. Multi mor-
tales convenere, studio etiam videndae novae urbis,
maxime proximi quique, Caeninenses, Crustumini, An-
9 temnates; etiam Sabinorum omnis multitudo cum liberis
ac coniugibus venit. Invitati hospitaliter per domos cum si-
tum moeniaque et frequentem tectis urbem vidissent, mi-
10 rantur tam brevi rem Romanam crevisse. Ubi spectaculi
tempus venit deditaeque eo mentes cum oculis erant, tum
ex composito orta vis, signoque dato iuventus Romana ad
11 rapiendas virgines discurrit. Magna pars forte, in quem
quaeque inciderat, raptae: quasdam forma excellentes pri-
moribus patrum destinatas ex plebe homines, quibus da-

their midst; and the envoys were frequently asked, on being dismissed, if they had opened a sanctuary for women as well as for men, for in that way only would they obtain suitable wives. This was a bitter insult to the young Romans, and the matter seemed certain to end in violence. Expressly to afford a fitting time and place for this, Romulus, concealing his resentment, made ready solemn games in honour of the equestrian Neptune, which he called Consualia.[1] He then bade proclaim the spectacle to the surrounding peoples, and his subjects prepared to celebrate it with all the resources within their knowledge and power, that they might cause the occasion to be noised abroad and eagerly expected. Many people—for they were also eager to see the new city—gathered for the festival, especially those who lived nearest, the inhabitants of Caenina, Crustumium, and Antemnae. The Sabines, too, came with all their people, including their children and wives. They were hospitably entertained in every house, and when they had looked at the site of the city, its walls, and its numerous buildings, they marvelled that Rome had so rapidly grown great. When the time came for the show, and people's thoughts and eyes were busy with it, the preconcerted attack began. At a given signal the young Romans darted this way and that, to seize and carry off the maidens. In most cases these were taken by the men in whose path they chanced to be. Some, of exceptional beauty, had been marked out for the chief senators, and

[1] The Consualia was a harvest festival, held on August 21. Consus, the true name of the god, is from condere, "to store up." From the association of the festival with horses came the later identification of the god with *Neptunus Equester*.

12   tum negotium erat, domos deferebant: unam longe ante
alias specie ac pulchritudine insignem a globo Thalassii
cuiusdam raptam ferunt, multisque sciscitantibus cuinam
eam ferrent, identidem, ne quis violaret, Thalassio ferri
13   clamitatum; inde nuptialem hanc vocem factam. Turbato
per metum ludicro maesti parentes virginum profugiunt,
incusantes violati hospitii scelus deumque invocantes,
cuius ad sollemne ludosque per fas ac fidem decepti venis-
14   sent. Nec raptis aut spes de se melior aut indignatio est mi-
nor. Sed ipse Romulus circumibat docebatque patrum id
superbia factum, qui conubium finitimis negassent; illas
tamen in matrimonio, in societate fortunarum omnium ci-
vitatisque, et quo nihil carius humano generi sit, liberum
15   fore; mollirent modo iras et, quibus fors corpora dedisset,
darent animos. Saepe ex iniuria postmodum gratiam or-
tam, eoque melioribus usuras viris, quod adnisurus pro se
quisque sit ut, cum suam vicem functus officio sit, paren-
16   tium etiam patriaeque expleat desiderium. Accedebant
blanditiae virorum factum purgantium cupiditate atque
amore, quae maxime ad muliebre ingenium efficaces
preces sunt.

were carried off to their houses by plebeians to whom the
office had been entrusted. One, who far excelled the rest
in mien and loveliness, was seized, the story relates, by
the gang of a certain Thalassius. Being repeatedly asked
for whom they were bearing her off, they kept shouting
that no one should touch her, for they were taking her to
Thalassius, and this was the origin of the wedding-cry.[1]
The sports broke up in a panic, and the parents of the
maidens fled sorrowing. They charged the Romans with
the crime of violating hospitality, and invoked the gods to
whose solemn games they had come, deceived in violation
of religion and honour. The stolen maidens were no more
hopeful of their plight, nor less indignant. But Romulus
himself went amongst them and explained that the pride of
their parents had caused this deed, when they had refused
their neighbours the right to intermarry; nevertheless the
daughters should be wedded and become co-partners in
all the possessions of the Romans, in their citizenship and,
dearest privilege of all to the human race, in their children;
only let them moderate their anger, and give their hearts to
those to whom fortune had given their persons. A sense of
injury had often given place to affection, and they would
find their husbands the kinder for this reason, that every
man would earnestly endeavour not only to be a good hus-
band, but also to console his wife for the home and parents
she had lost. His arguments were seconded by the wooing
of the men, who excused their act on the score of passion
and love, the most moving of all pleas to a woman's heart.

[1] Plutarch, *Rom.* 15, also gives the story, and observes that the
Romans used "Talasius" as the Greeks did "Hymenaeus."

PROPERTIUS

Translation by G. P. Goold

I

Cynthia prima suis miserum me cepit ocellis,
    contactum nullis ante cupidinibus.
tum mihi constantis deiecit lumina fastus
    et caput impositis pressit Amor pedibus,
5 donec me docuit castas odisse puellas
    improbus, et nullo vivere consilio.
ei mihi, iam toto furor hic non deficit anno,
    cum tamen adversos cogor habere deos.

Milanion nullos fugiendo, Tulle, labores
10   saevitiam durae contudit Iasidos.
nam modo Partheniis amens errabat in antris,
    ibat et hirsutas saepe videre feras;
ille etiam Hylaei percussus vulnere rami
    saucius Arcadiis rupibus ingemuit.
15 ergo velocem potuit domuisse puellam:
    tantum in amore fides et benefacta valent.

Elegies 1.1, 1.4

Cynthia

Cynthia first with her eyes ensnared me, poor wretch,
that had previously been untouched by desire. It was then
that Love made me lower my looks of stubborn pride and
trod my head beneath his feet, until the villain taught me
to shun decent girls and to lead the life of a ne'er-do-well.
Poor me, for a whole year now this frenzy has not abated,
while I am compelled to endure the frown of heaven.

It was, friend Tullus, by shrinking from no hardship
that Milanion broke down the cruelty of harsh Atalanta.[1]
For now he wandered distraught in the Parthenian glens,
and now he would often go and look upon shaggy wild
beasts. He was also dealt a wound from the club Hylaeus
bore, and on the rocks of Arcady he moaned in pain. Thus
he was able to subdue the swift-footed girl: such power in
love have devotion and service.

[1] It is especially characteristic of Propertius that he dignifies
his love by relating it to mythology, thus endowing it with a time-
less splendour.

in me tardus Amor non ullas cogitat artes,
    nec meminit notas, ut prius, ire vias.
at vos, deductae quibus est pellacia lunae
20   et labor in magicis sacra piare focis,
en agedum dominae mentem convertite nostrae,
    et facite illa meo palleat ore magis!
tunc ego crediderim Manes et sidera vobis
    posse Cytinaeis ducere carminibus.

25 aut vos, qui sero lapsum revocatis, amici,
    quaerite non sani pectoris auxilia.
fortiter et ferrum saevos patiemur et ignes,
    sit modo libertas quae velit ira loqui.
ferte per extremas gentes et ferte per undas,
30   qua non ulla meum femina norit iter.

vos remanete, quibus facili deus annuit aure,
    sitis et in tuto semper amore pares.
nam me nostra Venus noctes exercet amaras,
    et nullo vacuus tempore defit Amor.
35 hoc, moneo, vitate malum: sua quemque moretur
    cura, neque assueto mutet amore torum.
quod si quis monitis tardas adverterit aures,
    heu referet quanto verba dolore mea!

IV

Quid mihi tam multas laudando, Basse, puellas
    mutatum domina cogis abire mea?
quid me non pateris vitae quodcumque sequetur
    hoc magis assueto ducere servitio?

In my case dull-witted Love thinks up no stratagems, and remembers not to tread, as formerly, his well-known paths. But you, whose practice it is to lure the Moon down from the sky and to propitiate spirits over the magic fire, come, alter the heart of my mistress and see that she turn paler than this cheek of mine. Then should I credit you with the power of summoning ghosts and stars with Thessalian spells.

Else you, my friends, who too late call back the fallen, seek medicines for a heart that is sick. I shall bravely submit to the knife and cautery, if only I were free to utter the promptings of anger. Carry me through distant lands and over distant seas, where no woman may know my path.

Stay you at home, to whose prayer the god has nodded with easy ear, and be ever paired in a safe love. For I am harassed by our goddess Venus through nights of torment, and Cupid is never idle, never absent. Shun this plague, I counsel you: let everyone cling to his own sweetheart, nor switch his affections when love has grown familiar. But if anyone turn a deaf ear to my warning, ah, with what pain shall he recall my words!

To Bassus: a rebuke

Why, Bassus,[2] by praising so many other girls do you press me to change and forsake my mistress? Why do you not rather let me spend whatever time I have left to live in bondage I have grown used to?

---

[2] Although Bassus is named only in this poem, he was a real person, who with Ponticus and Ovid formed part of Propertius' literary circle.

5   tu licet Antiopae formam Nycteidos, et tu
       Spartanae referas laudibus Hermionae,
    et quascumque tulit formosi temporis aetas;
       Cynthia non illas nomen habere sinat:
    nedum, si levibus fuerit collata figuris,
10   inferior duro iudice turpis eat.

    haec sed forma mei pars est extrema furoris;
       sunt maiora, quibus, Basse, perire iuvat:
    ingenuus color et motis decor artubus et quae
       gaudia sub tacita discere veste libet.
15   quo magis et nostros contendis solvere amores,
       hoc magis accepta fallit uterque fide.

    non impune feres: sciet haec insana puella
       et tibi non tacitis vocibus hostis erit;
    nec tibi me post haec committet Cynthia nec te
20   quaeret; erit tanti criminis illa memor,
    et te circum omnis alias irata puellas
       differet: heu nullo limine carus eris.

    nullas illa suis contemnet fletibus aras,
       et quicumque sacer, qualis ubique, lapis.
25   non ullo gravius temptatur Cynthia damno
       quam sibi cum rapto cessat amore decus,
    praecipue nostro. maneat sic semper, adoro,
       nec quicquam ex illa quod querar inveniam!

5.1   invide, tu tandem voces compesce molestas
  2   et sine nos cursu, quo sumus, ire pares!

Though your praises recall the loveliness of Antiope, Nycteus' child, and of Spartan Hermione, and all the women the years of the age of beauty produced: Cynthia would make their glory pale. Much less, if compared with trivial beauties, need she fear the disgrace of being pronounced inferior even by a fastidious judge.

Yet this beauty is the least part of my frenzy; she has greater charms, Bassus, which I am glad to lose my head over: her well-bred complexion, her grace when she moves her limbs, and thrills I love to experience beneath the secrecy of the coverlet. And the more you endeavour to undo our love, the more each of us foils you through the pledge which is cherished.

You will not get away with it: my furious sweetheart will hear of this and be your foe with no unspoken words; nor hereafter will Cynthia entrust me to you or seek you out (she will not forget such a dire offence), and in her anger she will discredit you with all other girls: woe to you: no doorstep will welcome you then.

No altar will be too mean to receive her tears, or whatever sacred stone there is, no matter of what kind and where. No loss more keenly provokes Cynthia than when love has been stolen from her and her charms lie idle, especially when that love is mine. May she ever thus remain, I pray, and may I find nothing in her of which to complain!

Envious man, curb now at last your tiresome tongue and leave the pair of us to proceed on our way together!

OVID

Translation by Grant Showerman;
revised by G. P. Goold

Nec quia te nostra sperem prece posse moveri,
    adloquor—adverso movimus ista deo;
5 sed merita et famam corpusque animumque pudicum
    cum male perdiderim, perdere verba leve est.
Certus es ire tamen miseramque relinquere Dido,
    atque idem venti vela fidemque ferent?
certus es, Aenea, cum foedere solvere naves,
10   quaeque ubi sint nescis, Itala regna sequi?
nec nova Carthago, nec te crescentia tangunt
    moenia nec sceptro tradita summa tuo?
facta fugis, facienda petis; quaerenda per orbem
    altera, quaesita est altera terra tibi.
15 ut terram invenias, quis eam tibi tradet habendam?
    quis sua non notis arva tenenda dabit?

---

1 Ovid has the fourth book of the *Aeneid* in mind as he composes this letter.

Heroines 7.3–44

A fictional letter from Dido to Aeneas

DIDO TO AENEAS

Not because I hope you may be moved by prayer of mine do I address you—for with God's will adverse I have begun the words you read; but because, after wretched losing of desert, of reputation, and of purity of body and soul, the losing of words is a matter slight indeed.

Are you resolved none the less to go, and to abandon wretched Dido,[1] and shall the same winds bear away from me at once your sails and your promises? Are you resolved, Aeneas, to break at the same time from your moorings and from your pledge, and to follow after the fleeting realms of Italy, which lie you know not where? and does new-founded Carthage not touch you, nor her rising walls, nor the sceptre of supreme power placed in your hand? What is achieved, you turn your back upon; what is to be achieved, you ever pursue. One land has been sought and gained, and ever must another be sought, through the wide world. Yet, even should you find the land of your desire, who will give it over to you for your own? Who will deliver his fields to unknown hands to keep? I suppose a sec-

175

scilicet alter amor tibi restat et altera Dido;
    quamque iterum fallas altera danda fides.
quando erit, ut condas instar Carthaginis urbem
20   et videas populos altus ab arce tuos?
omnia ut eveniant, nec te tua vota morentur,
    unde tibi, quae te sic amet, uxor erit?
Uror, ut inducto ceratae sulpure taedae,
    ut pia fumosis addita tura focis.
25 Aeneas, oculis semper vigilantis inhaeret;
    Aenean animo noxque quiesque refert.
ille quidem male gratus et ad mea munera surdus,
    et quo, si non sim stulta, carere velim;
non tamen Aenean, quamvis male cogitat, odi,
30   sed queror infidum questaque peius amo.
parce, Venus, nurui, durumque amplectere fratrem,
    frater Amor, castris militet ille tuis!
aut ego, quae coepi, (neque enim dedignor) amorem,
    materiam curae praebeat ille meae!
35 Fallor, et ista mihi falso iactatur imago;
    matris ab ingenio dissidet ille suae.
te lapis et montes innataque rupibus altis
    robora, te saevae progenuere ferae,
aut mare, quale vides agitari nunc quoque ventis,
40   qua tamen adversis fluctibus ire paras.
quo fugis ? obstat hiemps. hiemis mihi gratia prosit!
    adspice, ut eversas concitet Eurus aquas!
quod tibi malueram, sine me debere procellis;
    iustior est animo ventus et unda tuo.

ond love lies in store for you, and a second Dido; a second pledge to give, and a second time to prove false. When will it be your fortune, think you, to found a city like to Carthage, and from the citadel on high to look down upon peoples of your own? Should your every wish be granted, even should you meet with no delay in the answering of your prayers, whence will come the wife to love you as I?

I am all ablaze with love, like torches of wax tipped with sulphur, like pious incense placed on smoking altar-fires. Aeneas my eyes cling to through all my waking hours; Aeneas is in my heart throughout the stillness of the night. 'Tis true he is an ingrate, and unresponsive to my kindnesses, and were I not fond I should be willing to have him go; yet, however ill his thought of me, I hate him not, but only complain of his faithlessness, and when I have complained I do but love more madly still. Spare, O Venus, the bride of thy son; lay hold of thy hard-hearted brother, O brother Love, and make him to serve in thy camp! Or let me who started (and I feel no shame at having done so) supply the love and he the fuel for my affection.

Ah, vain delusion! the fancy that flits before my mind is not the truth; far different his heart from his mother's. Of rocks and mountains were you begotten, and of the oak sprung from the lofty cliff, of savage wild beasts, or of the sea—such a sea as even now you look upon, tossed by the winds, by which you are preparing your departure, despite the threatening floods. Whither are you flying? The tempest rises to stay you. Let the tempest be my grace! Look you, how Eurus tosses the rolling waters! What I had preferred to owe to you, let me owe to the stormy blasts; wind and wave are juster than your heart.

MANILIUS

Translation by G. P. Goold

Haec ego divino cupiam cum ad sidera flatu
ferre, nec in turba nec turbae carmina condam,
sed solus, vacuo veluti vectatus in orbe
liber agam currus non occursantibus ullis
140 nec per iter socios commune regentibus actus,
sed caelo noscenda canam, mirantibus astris
et gaudente sui mundo per carmina vatis,
vel quibus illa sacros non invidere meatus
notitiamque sui, minima est quae turba per orbem.
145 illa frequens, quae divitias, quae diligit aurum,
imperia et fasces mollemque per otia luxum
et blandis diversa sonis dulcemque per aures
affectum, ut modico noscenda ad fata labore.
hoc quoque fatorum est, legem perdiscere fati.
150   Et primum astrorum varia est natura notanda
carminibus per utrumque genus. nam mascula sex sunt,

Characteristics of the signs of the zodiac

This is the theme I should wish with breath inspired to carry to the stars. Not in the crowd nor for the crowd shall I compose my song, but alone, as though borne round an empty circuit I were freely driving my car with none to cross my path or steer a course beside me over a common route, I shall sing it for the skies to hear, while the stars marvel and the firmament rejoices in the song of its bard, and for those to whom the stars have not grudged knowledge of themselves and their sacred motions, the smallest society on earth. Vast is the crowd which worships wealth and gold, power and the trappings of office, soft luxury amid ease, diversions of seductive music, and a happy feeling stealing through the ears, objects of slight labour compared with the understanding of fate. Yet this too is the gift of fate, the will to learn fate's laws.

My song must first mark the differing nature of the signs[1] according to sex. For six are masculine, whilst as

[1] Henceforth throughout the *Astronomica* "signs" will usually mean the signs of the zodiac.

diversi totidem generis sub principe Tauro:
cernis ut aversos redeundo surgat in artus.
alternant genus et vicibus variantur in orbem.
155   Humanas etiam species in parte videbis,
nec mores distant: pecudum pars atque ferarum
ingenium facient. quaedam signanda sagaci
singula sunt animo, propria quae sorte feruntur:
nunc binis insiste; dabunt geminata potentis
160 per socium effectus. multum comes addit et aufert,
ambiguisque valent, quis sunt collegia, fatis
ad meritum noxamque. duos per sidera Pisces
et totidem Geminos nudatis aspice membris.
his coniuncta manent alterno bracchia nexu,
165 dissimile est illis iter in contraria versis.
par numerus, sed enim dispar natura notanda est.
atque haec ex paribus toto gaudentia censu
signa meant, nihil exterius mirantur in ipsis
amissumve dolent, quaedam quod, parte recisa
170 atque ex diverso commissis corpore membris,
ut Capricornus et intentum qui derigit arcum
iunctus equo: pars huic hominis, sed nulla priori.

180

many, led by the Bull, are of the opposite sex: you see how he rises by his hind limbs when he reappears. They alternate their sex, changing one after another round the circle.[2]

You will also behold the human form in some, and the dispositions they bestow are not out of keeping; some will produce the nature of cattle and beasts.[3] Certain signs must with careful mind be noted as single, and these keep to an unshared estate.[4] Now turn to the double signs; being doubled they will exert influences the power of which is tempered by a partner. Much does a companion add and take away, and the signs that are accompanied are powerful for good or ill, dispensing doubtful destinies. Look among the constellations for the two Fishes and Twins of like number with limbs unclad. The arms of the Twins are for ever linked in mutual embrace; but the Fishes face opposite ways and have different courses. Mark well that, though the two signs are alike in their duality, they are unlike in their nature. These are they that of the double signs go rejoicing in a full estate and wonder at nothing foreign in themselves or mourn for aught lost, as do certain signs of amputated limb and members put together from unlike bodies, as Capricorn and he that joined to a horse takes aim with taut bow: the latter has part that is man, but the

---

[2] Thus masculine are ♈ ♊ ♌ ♎ ♐ ♒; feminine ♉ ♋ ♍ ♏ ♓ ♓.

[3] Human: ♊ ♍ ♒; bestial: ♈ ♉ ♋ ♌ ♏ ♑ ♓ . Of the others ♎ is implied at 2. 528 to be human, while ♐ plainly combines both natures.

[4] Single: ♈ ♉ ♋ ♌ ♎ ♏ ♒.

[hoc quoque servandum est alta discrimen in arte,
distat enim gemini duo sint duplane figura]
175 quin etiam Erigone binis numeratur in astris,
nec facies ratio duplex; nam desinit aestas,
incipit autumnus media sub Virgine utrimque.
idcirco tropicis praecedunt omnibus astra
bina, ut Lanigero, Chelis Cancroque Caproque,
180 quod duplicis retinent conexo tempore vires.
ut, quos subsequitur Cancer per sidera fratres,
e geminis alter florentia tempora veris
sufficit, aestatem sitientem provehit alter;
nudus uterque tamen, sentit quia uterque calorem,
185 ille senescentis veris, subeuntis at ille
aestatis : par est primae sors ultima parti.
quin etiam Arcitenens, qui te, Capricorne, sub ipso
promittit, duplici formatus imagine fertur:
mitior autumnus mollis sibi vindicat artus
190 materiamque hominis, fera tergo membra rigentem
excipiunt hiemem mutantque in tempora signum.
quosque Aries prae se mittit, duo tempora Pisces
bina dicant: hiemem hic claudit, ver incohat alter.

former none.[5] Erigone, too, is numbered among the double signs, but the duality in her appearance [6] is not the reason; for at the middle of the Virgin summer on one side ceases and autumn on the other begins.[7] Double signs precede all the tropic ones,[8] the Ram, the Claws, the Crab, and the Sea-goat, for the reason that, linking season with season, they possess double powers. Just as one of the twin brothers followed by the Crab round the zodiac imparts blossoming springtime, so the other brings on thirsting summer; yet each is unclad, for each feels the heat, the one of aging spring, the other of approaching summer: the last portion of the former is matched by the first degree of the latter. The Archer, too, who gives promise of Capricorn behind himself, comes shaped with twofold appearance: milder autumn claims the smooth limbs and body of his human allotment, whilst the animal portions in his rear prepare for frosty winter and change the sign to suit the change of season. And the two Fishes that the Ram sends before himself denote two seasons: one concludes winter,

[5] [173 f.]: "This distinction, too, must be preserved in our lofty art, for it makes a difference whether double signs are twin or of composite shape."

[6] She has two wings, and is so figured on the Farnese globe.

[7] Thus the double signs are ♊ ♍ ♐ ♑ ♓.

[8] The argument developed by the poet presupposes that the turning point of the seasons occurs in the *first* degree of the tropic signs. Notice that the term is applied to Aries and Libra (equinoctial signs) as well as Cancer and Capricorn, the signs properly tropic.

cum sol aequoreis revolans decurrit in astris,
195   hiberni coeunt cum vernis roribus imbres.
utraque sors umoris habet fluitantia signa.
     Quin tria signa novem signis coniuncta repugnant
et quasi seditio caelum tenet. aspice Taurum
clunibus et Geminos pedibus, testudine Cancrum
200   surgere, cum rectis oriantur cetera membris;
ne mirere moras, cum sol aversa per astra
aestivum tardis attollat mensibus annum.

the other introduces spring. When the returning[9] Sun courses through the watery stars,[10] then winter's rains mingle with showers of spring: each sort of moisture belongs in the double-sign that swims.

Further, three adjacent signs are at variance with the other nine and a kind of dissension takes hold of heaven. Observe that the Bull rises by his hind quarters, the Twins by their feet, the Crab by his shell, whereas all the others rise in upright posture;[11] so wonder not at the delay when in tardy months the Sun carries summertide aloft[12] through signs which rise hind-first.

[9] The Sun's annual orbit beginning in Aries.

[10] Pisces.

[11] Inverted: ♉ ♊ ♋ (all adjacent); upright: ♈ ♉ ♍ ♎ ♏ ♐ ♑ ♒ ♓.

[12] Aloft to the tropic of Cancer.

SENECA

Translation by John G. Fitch

Tellure rupta Tartaro gressum extuli,
Stygiam cruenta praeferens dextra facem
595   thalamis scelestis: nubat his flammis meo
Poppaea nato iuncta, quas vindex manus
dolorque matris vertet ad tristes rogos.
manet inter umbras impiae caedis mihi
semper memoria, manibus nostris gravis
600   adhuc inultis: reddita est meritis meis
funesta merces puppis et pretium imperi
nox illa qua naufragia deflevi mea.
comitum necem natique crudelis nefas
deflere votum fuerat: haud tempus datum est
605   lacrimis, sed ingens scelere geminavit nefas.
perempta ferro, foeda vulneribus sacros
intra penates spiritum effudi gravem
erepta pelago—sanguine extinxi meo
nec odia nati: saevit in nomen ferus
610   matris tyrannus, obrui meritum cupit,
simulacra, titulos destruit memores mei

186

Octavia 593–645

Agrippina, mother of Nero, returns from the underworld
to speak of her son's crimes

GHOST OF AGRIPPINA

Bursting through the earth I have made my way from
Tartarus, bearing a Stygian torch in my bloody hand to her-
ald this iniquitous wedding. Let Poppaea marry my son by
the light of these flames, which my hand of vengeance, my
anger as a mother, will turn to funeral fires. Even amidst
the dead the memory of that unnatural murder remains
with me always, and burdens my still unavenged shade: the
payment rendered for my services was that lethal ship; the
reward for imperial power, that night on which I wept over
my shipwreck. I would have wished to weep over my com-
panions' deaths and my cruel son's villainy, but no time was
given for tears: he renewed his great villainy with more
crime. Dispatched by the sword, befouled by wounds,
amidst the sanctities of my home I gave up my labouring
spirit, just rescued from the sea. Yet my blood did not
quench my son's hatred. The fierce tyrant rages against
his mother's name, wants my services obliterated, throws
down the statues and inscriptions that bear my memory

totum per orbem, quem dedit poenam in meam
puero regendum noster infelix amor.
  Extinctus umbras agitat infestus meas
615 flammisque vultus noxios coniunx petit,
instat, minatur, imputat fatum mihi
tumulumque nati, poscit auctorem necis.
iam parce: dabitur, tempus haud longum peto.
ultrix Erinys impio dignum parat
620 letum tyranno, verbera et turpem fugam
poenasque quîs et Tantali vincat sitim,
dirum laborem Sisyphi, Tityi alitem
Ixionisque membra rapientem rotam.
licet extruat marmoribus atque auro tegat
625 superbus aulam, limen armatae ducis
servent cohortes, mittat immensas opes
exhaustus orbis, supplices dextram petant
Parthi cruentam, regna divitias ferant,
veniet dies tempusque quo reddat suis
630 animam nocentem sceleribus, iugulum hostibus,
desertus ac destructus et cunctis egens.
  Heu, quo labor, quo vota ceciderunt mea!
quo te furor provexit attonitum tuus
et fata, nate, cedat ut tantis malis
635 genetricis ira, quae tuo scelere occidit!
utinam, antequam te parvulum in lucem edidi
aluique, saevae nostra lacerassent ferae
viscera: sine ullo scelere, sine sensu innocens

throughout the world—the world that my ill-starred love gave him as a boy to rule, to my own harm.

My spirit is hounded fiercely by my dead husband; he thrusts burning brands at my guilty face, looms over me, threatens me, blames me for his death and his son's grave, and demands his murderer.[36] Wait—he will be provided, I need only a little time! The avenging Erinys is planning a worthy death for that unnatural tyrant: lashes, and shameful flight, and torments to surpass the thirst of Tantalus, Sisyphus' dreadful labour, the vulture of Tityos, and the wheel that spins Ixion's limbs. Though he may pile up a palace of marble and cover it with gold[37] in his arrogance, though armed squadrons guard their commander's door, though the depleted world sends him its immense resources, though Parthians seek to kiss his bloody hand in supplication, though kingdoms bring him their riches, there will come a day and time when he will pay for his crimes with his guilty spirit and pay his enemies with his throat, deserted and thrown down and utterly destitute.

Oh, how far my labours and prayers have fallen! How far your wild madness and your destiny have brought you, son—to a point where your mother's anger fades before such disasters, though she died by your crime. I wish that before I brought you into the light as a tiny baby and suckled you, wild beasts had ripped apart my womb! You would have died my innocent child, free of crime and conscious-

---

[36] The son is Britannicus, his murderer Nero. Probably Agrippina sees or imagines Claudius' ghost before her (cf. Medea's vision at *Med* 958–966); or she may mean that Claudius attacks her in the underworld.   [37] A prophetic reference to Nero's lavish Golden House, begun in A.D. 64.

meus occidisses; iunctus atque haerens mihi
640   semper quieta cerneres sede inferum
proavos patremque, nominis magni viros—
quos nunc pudor luctusque perpetuus manet
ex te, nefande, meque quae talem tuli.
      Quid tegere cesso Tartaro vultus meos,
645   noverca coniunx mater infelix meis?

ness; clinging close to me in a peaceful corner of the un-
derworld, you would have gazed forever on your father and
forefathers, men of great name—but now doomed to ever-
lasting shame and grief by you (so evil!) and by me who
bore such a son.

Why am I slow to hide my face in Tartarus, I who blight
my kin as stepmother, wife, and mother?

PLINY

Translation by H. Rackham

79   Verum omnes prius genitos futurosque postea supera-
vit Apelles Cous olympiade centesima duodecima. pic-
turae plura solus prope quam ceteri omnes contulit, volu-
minibus etiam editis, quae doctrinam eam continent.
praecipua eius in arte venustas fuit, cum eadem aetate
maximi pictores essent; quorum opera cum admiraretur,
omnibus conlaudatis deesse illam suam venerem dicebat,
quam Graeci χάριτα vocant; cetera omnia contigisse, sed
80 hac sola sibi neminem parem. et aliam gloriam usurpavit,
cum Protogenis opus inmensi laboris ac curae supra mo-
dum anxiae miraretur; dixit enim omnia sibi cum illo paria

Natural History 35.36.79–87

On Apelles, considered the greatest painter of antiquity

But it was Apelles of Cos[1] who surpassed all the paint-
ers that preceded and all who were to come after him; he
dates in the 112th Olympiad.[2] He singly contributed al-
most more to painting than all the other artists put to-
gether, also publishing volumes containing the principles
of painting. His art was unrivalled for graceful charm, al-
though other very great painters were his contemporaries.
Although he admired their works and gave high praise to
all of them, he used to say that they lacked the glamour that
his work possessed, the quality denoted by the Greek word
charis, and that although they had every other merit, in
that alone no one was his rival. He also asserted another
claim to distinction when he expressed his admiration for
the immensely laborious and infinitely meticulous work of
Protogenes; for he said that in all respects his achieve-
ments and those of Protogenes were on a level, or those

[1] Really of Ephesus, but some of his famous works were at
Cos.
[2] 332–329 B.C.

esse aut illi meliora, sed uno se praestare, quod manum de
tabula sciret tollere, memorabili praecepto nocere saepe
nimiam diligentiam. fuit autem non minoris simplicitatis
quam artis. Melanthio dispositione cedebat, Asclepiodoro
de mensuris, hoc est quanto quid a quoque distare debe-
ret.

81   Scitum inter Protogenen et eum quod accidit. ille
Rhodi vivebat, quo cum Apelles adnavigasset, avidus
cognoscendi opera eius fama tantum sibi cogniti, continuo
officinam petiit. aberat ipse, sed tabulam amplae
magnitudinis in machina aptatam una custodiebat anus.
haec foris esse Protogenen respondit interrogavitque, a
quo quaesitum diceret. 'ab hoc,' inquit Apelles adreptoque
penicillo lineam ex colore duxit summae tenuitatis per
82 tabulam. et reverso Protogeni quae gesta erant anus
indicavit. ferunt   artificem   protinus   contemplatum
subtilitatem dixisse Apellen venisse, non cadere in alium
tam absolutum opus; ipsumque alio colore tenuiorem
lineam in ipsa illa duxisse abeuntemque praecepisse, si
redisset ille, ostenderet adiceretque hunc esse quem
quaereret. atque ita evenit. revertit enim Apelles et vinci
erubescens tertio colore lineas secuit nullum relinquens
83 amplius subtilitati locum. at Protogenes victum se

of Protogenes were superior, but that in one respect he
stood higher, that he knew when to take his hand away
from a picture—a noteworthy warning of the frequently
evil effects of excessive diligence. The candour of Apelles
was however equal to his artistic skill: he used to ac-
knowledge his inferiority to Melanthius in grouping, and
to Asclepiodorus in nicety of measurement, that is in the
proper space to be left between one object and another.

A clever incident took place between Protogenes and
Apelles. Protogenes lived at Rhodes, and Apelles made the
voyage there from a desire to make himself acquainted
with Protogenes's works, as that artist was hitherto only
known to him by reputation. He went at once to his studio.
The artist was not there but there was a panel of consider-
able size on the easel prepared for painting, which was in
the charge of a single old woman. In answer to his en-
quiry, she told him that Protogenes was not at home, and
asked who it was she should report as having wished to see
him. ' Say it was this person,' said Apelles, and taking up a
brush he painted in colour across the panel an extremely
fine line; and when Protogenes returned the old woman
showed him what had taken place. The story goes that the
artist, after looking closely at the finish of this, said that the
new arrival was Apelles, as so perfect a piece of work tal-
lied with nobody else; and he himself, using another col-
our, drew a still finer line exactly on the top of the first one,
and leaving the room told the attendant to show it to the
visitor if he returned and add that this was the person he
was in search of; and so it happened; for Apelles came
back, and, ashamed to be beaten, cut the lines with an-
other in a third colour, leaving no room for any further dis-
play of minute work. Hereupon Protogenes admitted he

confessus in portum devolavit hospitem quaerens,
placuitque sic eam tabulam posteris tradi omnium
quidem, sed artificum praecipuo miraculo. consumptam
eam priore incendio Caesaris domus in Palatio audio,
spectatam nobis ante, spatiose nihil aliud continentem
quam lineas visum effugientes, inter egregia multorum
opera inani similem et eo ipso allicientem omnique opere
nobiliorem.

84 Apelli fuit alioqui perpetua consuetudo numquam tam
occupatum diem agendi, ut non lineam ducendo exerceret
artem, quod ab eo in proverbium venit. idem perfecta op-
era proponebat in pergula transeuntibus atque, ipse post
tabulam latens, vitia quae notarentur auscultabat, vulgum
85 diligentiorem iudicem quam se praeferens; feruntque
reprehensum a sutore, quod in crepidis una pauciores
intus fecisset ansas, eodem postero die superbo
emendatione pristinae admonitionis cavillante circa crus,
indignatum prospexisse denuntiantem, ne supra crepidam
sutor iudicaret, quod et ipsum in proverbium abiit. fuit
enim et comitas illi, propter quam gratior Alexandro

was defeated, and flew down to the harbour to look for the visitor; and he decided that the panel should be handed on to posterity as it was, to be admired as a marvel by everybody, but particularly by artists. I am informed that it was burnt in the first fire which occurred in Caesar's palace on the Palatine; it had been previously much admired by us, on its vast surface containing nothing else than the almost invisible lines, so that among the outstanding works of many artists it looked like a blank space, and by that very fact attracted attention and was more esteemed than any masterpiece.

Moreover it was a regular custom with Apelles never to let a day of business to be so fully occupied that he did not practise his art by drawing a line,[3] which has passed from him into a proverb.[4] Another habit of his was when he had finished his works to place them in a gallery in the view of passers by, and he himself stood out of sight behind the picture and listened to hear what faults were noticed, rating the public as a more observant critic than himself. And it is said that he was found fault with by a shoemaker because in drawing a subject's sandals he had represented the loops in them as one too few, and the next day the same critic was so proud of the artist's correcting the fault indicated by his previous objection that he found fault with the leg, but Apelles indignantly looked out from behind the picture and rebuked him, saying that a shoemaker in his criticism must not go beyond the sandal—a remark that has also passed into a proverb. In fact he also possessed great courtesy of manners, which made him more agree-

[3] Probably an outline of some object.
[4] *Nulla dies sine linea*, 'No day without a line.'

PLINY

Magno frequenter in officinam ventitanti—nam, ut
diximus, ab alio se pingi vetuerat edicto—sed in officina
imperite multa disserenti silentium comiter suadebat,
86 rideri eum dicens a pueris, qui colores tererent. tantum
erat auctoritati iuris in regem alioqui iracundum.
quamquam Alexander honorem ei clarissimo perhibuit
exemplo. namque cum dilectam sibi e pallacis suis
praecipue, nomine Pancaspen, nudam pingi ob admira-
tionem formae ab Apelle iussisset eumque, dum paret,
captum amore sensisset, dono dedit ei, magnus animo,
maior imperio sui nec minor hoc facto quam victoria
87 alia, quia ipse se vicit, nec torum tantum suum, sed etiam
adfectum donavit artifici, ne dilectae quidem respectu
motus, cum modo regis ea fuisset, modo pictoris esset.
sunt qui Venerem anadyomenen ab illo pictam exemplari
putent.

able to Alexander the Great, who frequently visited his studio—for, as we have said, Alexander had published an edict forbidding any other artist to paint his portrait; but in the studio Alexander used to talk a great deal about painting without any real knowledge of it, and Apelles would politely advise him to drop the subject, saying that the boys engaged in grinding the colours were laughing at him: so much power did his authority exercise over a King who was otherwise of an irascible temper. And yet Alexander conferred honour on him in a most conspicuous instance; he had such an admiration for the beauty of his favourite mistress, named Pancaspe, that he gave orders that she should be painted in the nude by Apelles, and then discovering that the artist while executing the commission had fallen in love with the woman, he presented her to him, great-minded as he was and still greater owing to his control of himself, and of a greatness proved by this action as much as by any other victory: because he conquered himself, and presented not only his bedmate but his affection also to the artist, and was not even influenced by regard for the feelings of his favourite in having been recently the mistress of a monarch and now belonged to a painter. Some persons believe that she was the model from which the Aphrodite Anadyomene (Rising from the Sea) was painted.

PETRONIUS

Translation by Michael Heseltine;
revised by E. H. Warmington

Tandem ergo discubuimus pueris Alexandrinis aquam in manus nivatam infundentibus aliisque insequentibus ad pedes ac paronychia cum ingenti subtilitate tollentibus. Ac ne in hoc quidem tam molesto tacebant officio, sed obiter cantabant. Ego experiri volui, an tota familia cantaret, itaque potionem poposci. Paratissimus puer non minus me acido cantico excepit, et quisquis aliquid rogatus erat ut daret . . . pantomimi chorum, non patris familiae triclinium crederes. Allata est tamen gustatio valde lauta; nam iam omnes discubuerant praeter ipsum Trimalchionem, cui locus novo more primus servabatur. Ceterum in promulsidari asellus erat Corinthius cum bisaccio positus, qui habebat olivas in altera parte albas, in altera nigras. Tegebant asellum duae lances, in quarum marginibus nomen Trimalchionis inscriptum erat et argenti pondus. Ponticuli etiam ferruminati sustinebat glires melle ac papavere sparsos. Fuerunt et tomacula super craticulam argenteam fer-

Satyricon 31–33

At Trimalchio's dinner

At last then we sat down, and boys from Alexandria poured water cooled with snow over our hands. Others followed and knelt down at our feet, and proceeded with great skill to pare our hangnails. Even this unpleasant duty did not silence them, but they kept singing at their work. I wanted to find out whether the whole household could sing, so I asked for a drink. A ready slave repeated my order in a chant not less shrill. They all did the same if they were asked to hand anything. It was more like an actor's dance than a gentleman's dining-room. But some rich and tasty whets for the appetite were brought on; for every one had now sat down except Trimalchio, who had the first place kept for him in the new style. A donkey in Corinthian bronze stood on the side-board, with panniers holding olives, white in one side, black in the other. Two dishes hid the donkey; Trimalchio's name and their weight in silver was engraved on their edges. There were also dormice rolled in honey and poppy-seed, and supported on little bridges soldered to the plate. Then there were hot sau-

ventia posita, et infra craticulam Syriaca pruna cum granis
Punici mali.

32   In his eramus lautitiis, cum ipse Trimalchio ad
symphoniam allatus est positusque inter cervicalia
minutissima expressit imprudentibus risum. Pallio enim
coccineo adrasum excluserat caput circaque oneratas veste
cervices laticlaviam immiserat mappam fimbriis hinc
atque illinc pendentibus. Habebat etiam in minimo digito
sinistrae manus anulum grandem subauratum, extremo
vero articulo digiti sequentis minorem, ut mihi videbatur,
totum   aureum,   sed   plane   ferreis   veluti   stellis
ferruminatum. Et ne has tantum ostenderet divitias,
dextrum nudavit lacertum armilla aurea cultum et eboreo
33   circulo   lamina splendente conexo. Ut deinde pinna
argentea dentes perfodit, "Amici" inquit "nondum mihi
suave erat in triclinium venire, sed ne diutius absens
morae vobis essem, omnem voluptatem mihi negavi.
Permittitis tamen finiri lusum." Sequebatur puer cum ta-
bula terebinthina et crystallinis tesseris, notavique rem
omnium delicatissimam. Pro calculis enim albis ac nigris
aureos argenteosque habebat denarios. Interim dum ille
omnium textorum dicta inter lusum consumit, gustantibus
adhuc nobis repositorium allatum est cum corbe, in quo
gallina erat lignea patentibus in orbem alis, quales esse

sages laid on a silver grill, and under the grill damsons and seeds of pomegranate.

While we were engaged with these delicacies, Trimalchio was conducted in to the sound of music, propped on the tiniest of pillows. A laugh escaped the unwary. His head was shaven and peered out of a scarlet cloak, and over the heavy clothes on his neck he had put on a napkin with a broad stripe and fringes hanging from it all round. On the little finger of his left hand he had an enormous gilt ring, and on the top joint of the next finger a smaller ring which appeared to me to be entirely gold, but was really set all round with iron cut out in little stars.[1] Not content with this display of wealth, he bared his right arm, where a golden bracelet shone, and an ivory bangle clasped with a plate of bright metal. Then he said, as he picked his teeth with a silver quill, "It was not convenient for me to come to dinner yet, my friends, but I gave up all my own pleasure; I did not like to stay away any longer and keep you waiting. But you don't mind if I finish my game?" A boy followed him with a table of terebinth wood and two crystal dice, and I noticed the prettiest thing possible. Instead of black and white counters they used gold and silver coins. Trimalchio kept passing every kind of remark as he played, and we were still busy with the hors d'oeuvres, when a tray was brought in with a basket on it, in which there was a hen made of wood, spreading out her wings

[1] Petronius stresses the incongruous display of wealth by Trimalchio, who wears a gold ring as if he were an *eques*—and an iron one; he "sports" the broad (purple) stripe as if he were a senator—but on his napkin, not on his cloak; and his hair is cut close like a slave or a newly made freedman.

PETRONIUS

solent quae incubant ova. Accessere continuo duo servi et
symphonia strepente scrutari paleam coeperunt erutaque
subinde pavonina ova divisere convivis. Convertit ad hanc
scaenam Trimalchio vultum et "Amici" ait "pavonis ova
gallinae iussi supponi. Et mehercules timeo ne iam
concepti sint; temptemus tamen, si adhuc sorbilia sunt."
Accipimus nos cochlearia non minus selibras pendentia
ovaque ex farina pingui figurata pertundimus. Ego quidem
paene proieci partem meam, nam videbatur mihi iam
in pullum coisse. Deinde ut audivi veterem convivam:
"Hic nescio quid boni debet esse," persecutus putamen
manu pinguissimam ficedulam inveni piperato vitello
circumdatam.

as they do when they are sitting. The music grew loud: two slaves at once came up and then hunted in the straw. Peahen's eggs were pulled out and handed to the guests. Trimalchio turned towards this fine sight, and said, " I gave orders, my friends, that peahen's eggs should be put under a common hen. And upon my oath I am afraid they are addled by now. But we will try whether they are still fresh enough to suck." We took our spoons, half-a-pound in weight at least, and hammered at the eggs, which were balls of fine meal. I was on the point of throwing away my portion. I thought a peachick had already formed. But hearing a practised diner say, "What treasure have we here?" I poked through the shell with my finger, and found a very fat fig-eater,[1] rolled up in spiced yolk of egg.

[1] The name beccafico is applied in Italy to-day to several small passerine birds which frequent gardens in the autumn and sometimes peck at figs for insects and are eaten. The old Roman *ficedula* was probably one or more of these.

PLINY THE YOUNGER

Translation by Betty Radice

4   Erat Miseni classemque imperio praesens regebat. No-
num kal. Septembres hora fere septima mater mea indicat
ei adparere nubem inusitata et magnitudine et specie.
5   Usus ille sole, mox frigida, gustaverat iacens studebatque;
poscit soleas, ascendit locum ex quo maxime miraculum il-
lud conspici poterat. Nubes—incertum procul intuentibus
ex quo monte (Vesuvium fuisse postea cognitum est)—
oriebatur, cuius similitudinem et formam non alia magis
6   arbor quam pinus expresserit. Nam longissimo velut trun-
co elata in altum quibusdam ramis diffundebatur, credo
quia recenti spiritu evecta, dein senescente eo destituta
aut etiam pondere suo victa in latitudinem vanescebat,
candida interdum, interdum sordida et maculosa prout

Letters 6.16.4–20

Pliny the Elder, uncle of the letter-writer, observes the
eruption of Vesuvius in 79 A.D.

My uncle was stationed at Misenum,[1] in active com-
mand of the fleet. On 24 August, in the early afternoon, my
mother drew his attention to a cloud of unusual size and
appearance. He had been out in the sun, had taken a cold
bath, and lunched while lying down, and was then working
at his books. He called for his shoes and climbed up to a
place which would give him the best view of the phenome-
non. It was not clear at that distance from which moun-
tain the cloud was rising (it was afterwards known to be Ve-
suvius); its general appearance can best be expressed as
being like a pine[2] rather than any other tree, for it rose to
a great height on a sort of trunk and then split off into
branches, I imagine because it was thrust upwards by
the first blast and then left unsupported as the pressure
subsided, or else it was borne down by its own weight so
that it spread out and gradually dispersed. Sometimes it
looked white, sometimes blotched and dirty, according to

[1] The northern arm of the Bay of Naples (Capo Miseno).
[2] P. means the umbrella pine of the Mediterranean.

7   terram cineremve sustulerat. Magnum propiusque nos-
cendum ut eruditissimo viro visum. Iubet liburnicam apta-
ri; mihi si venire una vellem facit copiam; respondi studere
8   me malle, et forte ipse quod scriberem dederat. Egredie-
batur domo; accipit codicillos Rectinae Tasci imminenti
periculo exterritae (nam villa eius subiacebat, nec ulla nisi
9   navibus fuga): ut se tanto discrimini eriperet orabat. Vertit
ille consilium et quod studioso animo incohaverat obit
maximo. Deducit quadriremes, ascendit ipse non Rec-
tinae modo sed multis (erat enim frequens amoenitas
10   orae) laturus auxilium. Properat illuc unde alii fugiunt,
rectumque cursum recta gubernacula in periculum tenet
adeo solutus metu, ut omnes illius mali motus omnes figu-
ras ut deprenderat oculis dictaret enotaretque.
11   Iam navibus cinis incidebat, quo propius accederent,
calidior et densior; iam pumices etiam nigrique et ambusti
et fracti igne lapides; iam vadum subitum ruinaque montis
litora obstantia. Cunctatus paulum an retro flecteret, mox
gubernatori ut ita faceret monenti "Fortes" inquit "fortuna
12   iuvat: Pomponianum pete." Stabiis erat diremptus sinu

the amount of soil and ashes it carried with it. My uncle's scholarly acumen saw at once that it was important enough for a closer inspection, and he ordered a fast boat to be made ready, telling me I could come with him if I wished. I replied that I preferred to go on with my studies, and as it happened he had himself given me some writing to do.

As he was leaving the house he was handed a message from Rectina, wife of Tascius, whose house was at the foot of the mountain, so that escape was impossible except by boat. She was terrified by the danger threatening her and implored him to rescue her from her fate. He changed his plans, and what he had begun in a spirit of inquiry he completed as a hero. He gave orders for the warships to be launched and went on board himself with the intention of bringing help to many more people besides Rectina, for this lovely stretch of coast was thickly populated. He hurried to the place which everyone else was hastily leaving, steering his course straight for the danger zone. He was entirely fearless, describing each new movement and phase of the portent to be noted down exactly as he observed them. Ashes were already falling, hotter and thicker as the ships drew near, followed by bits of pumice and blackened stones, charred and cracked by the flames: then suddenly they were in shallow water, and the shore was blocked by the debris from the mountain. For a moment my uncle wondered whether to turn back, but when the helmsman advised this he refused, telling him that Fortune stood by the courageous[1] and they must make for Pomponianus at Stabiae.[2] He was cut off there by the

[1] Terence, *Phormio* 203.

[2] Stabiae was four miles S. of Pompeii.

medio (nam sensim circumactis curvatisque litoribus
mare infunditur); ibi quamquam nondum periculo
adpropinquante, conspicuo tamen et cum cresceret prox-
imo, sarcinas contulerat in naves, certus fugae si contrarius
ventus resedisset. Quo tunc avunculus meus secundissimo
invectus, complectitur trepidantem consolatur hortatur,
utque timorem eius sua securitate leniret, deferri in
balineum iubet; lotus accubat cenat, aut hilaris aut (quod
13   aeque magnum) similis hilari. Interim e Vesuvio monte
pluribus locis latissimae flammae altaque incendia
relucebant, quorum fulgor et claritas tenebris noctis
excitabatur. Ille agrestium trepidatione ignes relictos
desertasque villas per solitudinem ardere in remedium
formidinis dictitabat. Tum se quieti dedit et quievit
verissimo quidem somno; nam meatus animae, qui illi
propter amplitudinem corporis gravior et sonantior erat,
14   ab iis qui limini obversabantur audiebatur. Sed area ex qua
diaeta adibatur ita iam cinere mixtisque pumicibus oppleta
surrexerat, ut si longior in cubiculo mora, exitus negaretur.
Excitatus procedit, seque Pomponiano ceterisque qui
15   pervigilaverant reddit. In commune consultant, intra tecta

breadth of the bay (for the shore gradually curves round a basin filled by the sea) so that he was not as yet in danger, though it was clear that this would come nearer as it spread. Pomponianus had therefore already put his belongings on board ship, intending to escape if the contrary wind fell. This wind was of course full in my uncle's favour, and he was able to bring his ship in. He embraced his terrified friend, cheered and encouraged him, and thinking he could calm his fears by showing his own composure, gave orders that he was to be carried to the bathroom. After his bath he lay down and dined; he was quite cheerful, or at any rate he pretended he was, which was no less courageous.

Meanwhile on Mount Vesuvius broad sheets of fire and leaping flames blazed at several points, their bright glare emphasized by the darkness of night. My uncle tried to allay the fears of his companions by repeatedly declaring that these were nothing but bonfires left by the peasants in their terror, or else empty houses on fire in the districts they had abandoned. Then he went to rest and certainly slept, for as he was a stout man his breathing was rather loud and heavy and could be heard by people coming and going outside his door. By this time the courtyard giving access to his room was full of ashes mixed with pumice-stones, so that its level had risen, and if he had stayed in the room any longer he would never have got out.[1] He was wakened, came out and joined Pomponianus and the rest of the household who had sat up all night. They debated whether to stay indoors or take their chance in the

[1] Hence the many bodies found in the excavations at Pompeii.

subsistant an in aperto vagentur. Nam crebris vastisque
tremoribus tecta nutabant, et quasi emota sedibus suis
16 nunc huc nunc illuc abire aut referri videbantur. Sub dio
rursus quamquam levium exesorumque pumicum casus
metuebatur, quod tamen periculorum collatio elegit; et
apud illum quidem ratio rationem, apud alios timorem
timor vicit. Cervicalia capitibus imposita linteis con-
stringunt; id munimentum adversus incidentia fuit.
17 Iam dies alibi, illic nox omnibus noctibus nigrior
densiorque; quam tamen faces multae variaeque lumina
solvebant. Placuit egredi in litus, et ex proximo adspicere,
ecquid iam mare admitteret; quod adhuc vastum et
18 adversum permanebat. Ibi super abiectum linteum
recubans semel atque iterum frigidam aquam poposcit
hausitque. Deinde flammae flammarumque praenuntius
odor sulpuris alios in fugam vertunt, excitant illum.
19 Innitens servolis duobus adsurrexit et statim concidit, ut
ego colligo, crassiore caligine spiritu obstructo, clausoque
stomacho qui illi natura invalidus et angustus et frequenter
20 aestuans erat. Ubi dies redditus (is ab eo quem novissime
viderat tertius), corpus inventum integrum inlaesum
opertumque ut fuerat indutus: habitus corporis quiescenti
quam defuncto similior.

open, for the buildings were now shaking with violent shocks, and seemed to be swaying to and fro as if they were torn from their foundations. Outside on the other hand, there was the danger of falling pumice-stones, even though these were light and porous; however, after comparing the risks they chose the latter. In my uncle's case one reason outweighed the other, but for the others it was a choice of fears. As a protection against falling objects they put pillows on their heads tied down with cloths.

Elsewhere there was daylight by this time, but they were still in darkness, blacker and denser than any night that ever was, which they relieved by lighting torches and various kinds of lamp. My uncle decided to go down to the shore and investigate on the spot the possibility of any escape by sea, but he found the waves still wild and dangerous. A sheet was spread on the ground for him to lie down, and he repeatedly asked for cold water to drink. Then the flames and smell of sulphur which gave warning of the approaching fire drove the others to take flight and roused him to stand up. He stood leaning on two slaves and then suddenly collapsed, I imagine because the dense fumes choked his breathing by blocking his windpipe which was constitutionally weak and narrow and often inflamed. When daylight returned on the 26th—two days after the last day he had seen—his body was found intact and uninjured, still fully clothed and looking more like sleep than death.

JUVENAL

Translation by Susanna Morton Braund

Respice nunc alia ac diversa pericula noctis:
quod spatium tectis sublimibus unde cerebrum
270   testa ferit, quotiens rimosa et curta fenestris
vasa cadant, quanto percussum pondere signent
et laedant silicem. possis ignavus haberi
et subiti casus improvidus, ad cenam si
intestatus eas: adeo tot fata, quot illa
275   nocte patent vigiles te praetereunte fenestrae.
ergo optes votumque feras miserabile tecum,
ut sint contentae patulas defundere pelves.
ebrius ac petulans, quia nullum forte cecidit,
dat poenas, noctem patitur lugentis amicum
280   Pelidae, cubat in faciem, mox deinde supinus:
[ergo non aliter poterit dormire; quibusdam]
somnum rixa facit. sed quamvis improbus annis
atque mero fervens cavet hunc quem coccina laena
vitari iubet et comitum longissimus ordo,

Satires 3.268–322

On life in Rome

Now consider the various other dangers of the night. What a long way it is from the high roofs for a tile to hit your skull! How often cracked and leaky pots tumble down from the windows! What a smash when they strike the pavement, marking and damaging it! You could be thought careless and unaware of what can suddenly befall if you go out to dinner without having made your will. As you pass by at night, there are precisely as many causes of death as there are open windows watching you. So make a wish and a pathetic prayer as you go that they'll be content with emptying their shallow basins on you. The drunken thug is in agony from failing, by some chance, to attack anyone. He's going through a night like Pelides[51] had when he was grieving for his friend, lying on his face and now on his back again. It takes a brawl to make him sleep. But however insolent he is, seething with youth and unmixed wine, he keeps clear of the man with the warning signs of scarlet

---

[51] Achilles, son of Peleus, whose grief at the death of his friend Patroclus is described at Homer *Il.* 24.10–11.

285 multum praeterea flammarum et aenea lampas.
me, quem luna solet deducere vel breve lumen
candelae, cuius dispenso et tempero filum,
contemnit. miserae cognosce prohoemia rixae,
si rixa est, ubi tu pulsas, ego vapulo tantum.
290 stat contra starique iubet. parere necesse est;
nam quid agas, cum te furiosus cogat et idem
fortior? 'unde venis?' exclamat, 'cuius aceto,
cuius conche tumes? quis tecum sectile porrum
sutor et elixi vervecis labra comedit?
295 nil mihi respondes? aut dic aut accipe calcem.
ede ubi consistas: in qua te quaero proseucha?'
dicere si temptes aliquid tacitusve recedas,
tantumdem est: feriunt pariter, vadimonia deinde
irati faciunt. libertas pauperis haec est:
300 pulsatus rogat et pugnis concisus adorat
ut liceat paucis cum dentibus inde reverti.
nec tamen haec tantum metuas; nam qui spoliet te
non derit clausis domibus postquam omnis ubique
fixa catenatae siluit compago tabernae.
305 interdum et ferro subitus grassator agit rem:
armato quotiens tutae custode tenentur
et Pomptina palus et Gallinaria pinus,
sic inde huc omnes tamquam ad vivaria currunt.

cloak and long retinue of attendants plus plenty of torches and bronze lamps. But me he despises, as I go home escorted usually by the moon or by the short-lived light of a candle—its wick I regulate and tend. Here are the preliminaries to the pathetic brawl, if a brawl it is when you do the beating and I just take it. He stands facing me and tells me to stop. I've no choice but to obey. After all, what can you do when a lunatic forces you, and he's stronger as well? 'Where have you just been?' he yells. 'Whose sour wine and beans have blown you out? Which shoemaker has been eating spring onions and boiled sheep's head with you? Nothing to say? Tell me or you'll get a kicking! Say, where's your pitch? Which synagogue shall I look for you in?' Whether you try to say something or silently retreat, it's all the same. They beat you up just the same and then, still angry, they sue for assault.[52] This is a poor man's freedom: when he's been beaten and treated like a punchbag, he can beg and plead to be allowed to go home with a few teeth left. And this is not all you have to be afraid of. After the houses are locked, when all the shuttering on the shops has been chained and fastened and fallen silent, there'll still be someone who'd rob you. And sometimes a gangster will suddenly be at his business with his knife: whenever the Pomptine marsh and Gallinarian forest[53] are safely occupied by an armed patrol, they all race from there into

[52] A *vadimonium* is a guarantee that the defendant will appear in court at a future date.

[53] The Pontine marshes were near the coast of Latium between Circeii and Terracina; the Gallinarian forest was in the west of Campania between the river Vulturnus and Cumae. It was difficult to police the bands of gangsters that operated there.

qua fornace graves, qua non incude catenae?
310 maximus in vinclis ferri modus, ut timeas ne
vomer deficiat, ne marra et sarcula desint.
felices proavorum atavos, felicia dicas
saecula quae quondam sub regibus atque tribunis
viderunt uno contentam carcere Romam.
315   His alias poteram et pluris subnectere causas,
sed iumenta vocant et sol inclinat. eundum est;
nam mihi commota iamdudum mulio virga
adnuit. ergo vale nostri memor, et quotiens te
Roma tuo refici properantem reddet Aquino,
320 me quoque ad Helvinam Cererem vestramque Dianam
converte a Cumis saturarum ego, ni pudet illas,
auditor gelidos veniam caligatus in agros.

Rome as if to their feeding grounds. Is there a furnace or anvil anywhere that isn't weighed down with the making of chains? Most of our iron is turned into fetters. You should be worried about a shortage of ploughshares and a dearth of mattocks and hoes.[54] Fortunate were our distant ancestors, you'd say, and fortunate those once-upon-a-time generations under the kings and tribunes that saw a Rome satisfied with a single prison.

I could add plenty other reasons to these, but the beasts are calling and the sun is sloping. I must go: the muleteer has been waving to me with his whip for some time. So, goodbye. Don't forget me. And whenever Rome sends you hurrying back to your own Aquinum[55] for a break, invite me too from Cumae to visit Helvius' Ceres and your Diana.[56] I'll come to your cool countryside in my heavy boots and listen to your satires, if they're not embarrassed.

[54] For the cliche that in time of war ploughshares and other agricultural implements are melted down into swords, see Virg. *Georg.* 1.508, Ov. *Fast.* 1.699–700.

[55] A town in Latium on the Via Latina about 75 miles from Rome, often taken (not necessarily correctly) to indicate J.'s birthplace.

[56] A temple of Ceres built by the Helvii, a family prominent in this area. Ceres and Diana were goddesses of the countryside.

APULEIUS

Translation by J. Arthur Hanson

Iam primum omnibus laciniis se devestit Pamphile et
arcula quadam reclusa pyxides plusculas inde depromit, de
quis unius operculo remoto atque indidem egesta ungue-
dine diuque palmulis suis affricta ab imis unguibus sese to-
tam adusque summos capillos perlinit, multumque cum
lucerna secreto collocuta, membra tremulo succussu qua-
tit. Quis leniter fluctuantibus promicant molles plumulae,
crescunt et fortes pinnulae; duratur nasus incurvus, co-
guntur ungues adunci. Fit bubo Pamphile. Sic edito stri-
dore querulo iam sui periclitabunda paulatim terra resul-
tat; mox in altum sublimata forinsecus totis alis evolat. . .

24   Haec identidem asseverans summa cum trepidatione
irrepit cubiculum et pyxidem depromit arcula. Quam ego
amplexus ac deosculatus prius, utque mihi prosperis fave-
ret volatibus deprecatus, abiectis propere laciniis totis,
avide manus immersi et haurito plusculo cuncta corporis
mei membra perfricui. Iamque alternis conatibus libratis

Lucius, eager to experience being a bird,
resorts to witchcraft, with disastrous results

First Pamphile took off all her clothes. Then she
opened a box and removed several small jars from it. She
took the cover off one of these and scooped out some oint-
ment, which she massaged for some time between her
palms and then smeared all over her body from the tips of
her toenails to the top of her hair. After a long secret con-
versation with her lamp she began to shake her limbs in
a quivering tremor. While her body undulated smoothly,
soft down sprouted up through her skin, and strong wing-
feathers grew out; her nose hardened and curved, and her
toenails bent into hooks. Pamphile had become an owl. So
she let out a plaintive screech and began testing herself by
jumping off the ground a little at a time. Soon she soared
aloft and flew out of the house on full wing. . .

After repeating this recipe several times, she[1] crept   24
very nervously into the room and removed a jar from the
box. First I embraced and kissed the jar and prayed to it to
bless me with a lucky flight. Then I hastily threw off all my
clothes, greedily plunged my hand into the jar, pulled out a
largish daub, and rubbed my body all over. Next I spread

bracchiis in avem similem gestiebam. Nec ullae plumulae
nec usquam pinnulae, sed plane pili mei crassantur in se-
tas, et cutis tenella duratur in corium, et in extimis palmu-
lis perdito numero toti digiti coguntur in singulas ungulas,
et de spinae meae termino grandis cauda procedit. Iam fa-
cies enormis et os prolixum et nares hiantes et labiae pen-
dulae; sic et aures immodicis horripilant auctibus. Nec ul-
lum miserae reformationis video solacium, nisi quod mihi
25   iam nequeunti tenere Photidem natura crescebat. Ac dum
salutis inopia cuncta corporis mei considerans non avem
me sed asinum video, querens de facto Photidis, sed iam
humano gestu simul et voce privatus, quod solum pote-
ram, postrema deiecta labia, umidis tamen oculis obli-
quum respiciens ad illam tacitus expostulabam.

Quae ubi primum me talem aspexit, percussit faciem
suam manibus infestis et "Occisa sum misera!" clamavit.
"Me trepidatio simul et festinatio fefellit et pyxidum simili-
tudo decepit. Sed bene quod facilior reformationis huius
medela suppeditat. Nam rosis tantum demorsicatis exibis
asinum statimque in meum Lucium postliminio redibis.
Atque utinam vesperi de more nobis parassem corollas
aliquas, ne moram talem patereris vel noctis unius. Sed
primo diluculo remedium festinabitur tibi."

26   Sic illa maerebat. Ego vero, quamquam perfectus asi-
nus et pro Lucio iumentum, sensum tamen retinebam hu-
manum. Diu denique ac multum mecum ipse deliberavi

out my arms and pumped them alternately, trying hard to become a bird like Pamphile. No down appeared, not a single feather. Instead my body hair was thickening into bristles and my soft skin hardening into hide. At the ends of my palms my fingers were losing their number and being all compressed together into single hoofs, and from the end of my spine came forth a great tail. My face was immense now, mouth spread, nostrils gaping, lips sagging. My ears too grew immoderately long and bristly. I saw no consolation in my wretched metamorphosis except for the fact that, although I could not now embrace Photis, my generative organ was growing.

Helplessly I examined every part of my body and saw   25
that I was not a bird, but an ass. I wanted to complain about what Photis had done, but I lacked human gestures as well as words. Still, I did the only thing I could: I hung my lower lip, looked askance at her with moist eyes, and berated her in silence.

Her first reaction when she saw my condition was to strike her face violently with her hands and scream, "I am lost and done for! My nervousness and haste misled me, and the similarity of the jars fooled me. But luckily a very easy cure is available for this metamorphosis. All you have to do is take a bite of roses and you will depart from the ass and immediately return to be my own Lucius once again. I only wish I had fixed some garlands for us this evening as I usually do, and then you would not have to endure waiting even one night like this. But the remedy will be rushed to you at the first light of dawn."

So she lamented. For my part, although I was a com-   26
plete ass and a beast of burden instead of Lucius, I still retained my human intelligence; and so I held a long, earnest

223

an nequissimam facinerosissimamque illam feminam spissis calcibus feriens et mordicus appetens necare deberem. Sed ab incepto temerario melior me sententia revocavit, ne morte multata Photide salutares mihi suppetias rursus exstinguerem. Deiecto itaque et quassanti capite ac demussata temporali contumelia, durissimo casui meo serviens ad equum illum vectorem meum probissimum in stabulum concedo.

debate with myself concerning that utterly worthless and criminal woman. Should I kick her repeatedly with my hoofs, assault her with my teeth, and kill her? But that was a rash idea and better thinking brought me back to my senses, lest, by punishing Photis with death, I also destroy the assistance I needed for recovery. So, lowering and shaking my head, I silently swallowed my temporary humiliation, and accommodating myself to my harsh misfortune, I went off to the stable to join my horse, my most excellent mount.

JEROME

Translation by F. A. Wright

AD MARCELLAM

1. Ambrosius, quo chartas, sumptus, notarios ministrante tam innumerabiles libros vere Adamantius et noster Χαλκέντερος explicavit, in quadam epistula, quam ad eundem de Athenis scripserat, refert numquam se cibos Origene praesente sine lectione sumpsisse, nunquam venisse somnum, nisi e fratribus aliquis sacris litteris personaret, hoc diebus egisse vel noctibus, ut et lectio orationem susciperet et oratio lectionem.

2. Quid nos, ventris animalia, tale umquam fecimus? Quos si secunda hora legentes invenerit, oscitamus, manu

Letters 43

A letter extolling the simple country life,
written in 385 A.D.

TO MARCELLA
Ambrose,[1] who supplied Origen with parchment, mo-
ney, and copyists, and thus enabled our man of brass [2] and
adamant to bring out his innumerable books, in a letter
written to his friend from Athens, declares that he never
took a meal in Origen's company without something being
read, and that he never fell asleep save to the sound of
some brother's voice reciting the Scriptures aloud. Day
and night it was their habit to make reading follow upon
prayer, and prayer upon reading, without a break.

Do we, poor creatures of the belly, ever behave like
this? If we spend more than an hour in reading, you will
find us yawning and trying to restrain our boredom by rub-

---

[1] Not the great Bishop of Milan who lived a century after
Origen, but a friend of Origen.

[2] 'Chalkenteros,' 'the man with entrails of brass,' an epithet
usually applied to the Alexandrian scholar Didymus, because of
his unwearied industry, is here transferred to Origen, who was
sometimes called 'Adamantius,' probably for the same reason.

faciem defricantes continemus stomachum et quasi post
multum laborem mundialibus rursum negotiis occupa-
mur. Praetermitto prandia, quibus onerata mens premitur.
Pudet dicere de frequentia salutandi, qua aut ipsi cotidie
ad alios pergimus aut ad nos venientes ceteros expecta-
mus. Deinceps itur in verba, sermo teritur, lacerantur ab-
sentes, vita aliena describitur et mordentes invicem consu-
mimur ab invicem. Talis nos cibus et occupat et dimittit.
Cum vero amici recesserint, ratiocinia subputamus. Nunc
ira personam nobis leonis inponit, nunc cura superflua in
annos multos duratura praecogitat, nec recordamur evan-
gelii dicens: 'Stulte, hac nocte repetunt animum tuam a
te; quae autem praeparasti, cuius erunt?' Vestes non ad
usum tantum, sed ad delicias conquiruntur. Ubicumque
conpendium est, velocior pes, citus sermo, auris adtentior;
si damnum, ut saepe in re familiari accidere solet, fuerit
nuntiatum, vultus maerore deprimitur. Laetamur ad num-
mum, obolo contristamur. Unde, cum in uno homine ani-
morum tam diversa sit facies, propheta dominum depreca-
tur dicens: 'Domine, in civitate tua imaginem eorum
dissipa.' Cum enim ad imaginem et similitudinem Dei
conditi sumus, ex vitio nostro et personas nobis plurimas
superinducimus, et quomodo in theatralibus scaenis unus
atque idem histrio nunc Herculem robustus ostentat, nunc
mollis in Venerem frangitur, nunc tremulus in Cybelen, ita

bing our eyes; then, as though we had been hard at work, we plunge once more into worldly affairs. I say nothing of the heavy meals which crush such mental faculties as we possess. I am ashamed to speak of our numerous calls, going ourselves every day to other people's houses, or waiting for others to come to us. The guests arrive and talk begins: a brisk conversation is engaged: we tear to pieces those who are not there: other people's lives are described in detail: we bite and are ourselves bitten in turn. With this fare the company is kept busy, and so at last it disperses. When our friends have left us, we reckon up our accounts, now frowning over them like angry lions, now with useless care planning schemes for the distant future. We remember not the words of the Gospel: 'Thou fool, this night thy soul shall be required of thee: then whose shall those things be which thou hast provided?'[3] We buy clothes, not solely for use, but for display. When we see a chance of making money, we quicken our steps, we talk fast, we strain our ears. If we are told that we have lost, as often must happen in business, our face is clouded with sorrow. A penny makes us merry: a halfpenny makes us sad. Therefore, as the phases of one man's mind are so conflicting, the prophet prays to the Lord, saying: 'O Lord, in thy city scatter their image.'[4] For while we were created in God's image and likeness, by reason of our own perversity we hide ourselves behind changing masks, and as on the stage one and the same actor now figures as a brawny Hercules, and now relaxes into the softness of a Venus or the quivering tone of

[3] St. Luke, xii. 20.

[4] Psalm lxxiii. 20. A.V. has 'when thou awakest,' but R.V. gives 'in the city' in margin = *in civitate tua* of Vulgate (Psalm lxxii. 20).

et nos, qui, si mundi non essemus, odiremur a mundo, tot habemus personarum similitudines, quot peccata.

3. Quapropter, quia vitae multum iam spatium transivimus fluctuando et navis nostra nunc procellarum concussa turbine, nunc scopulorum inlisionibus perforata est, quam primum licet, quasi quemdam portum secreta ruris intremus. Ibi cibarius panis et holus nostris manibus inrigatum, lac, deliciae rusticanae, viles quidem, sed innocentes cibos praebeant. Ita viventes non ab oratione somnus, non saturitas a lectione revocabit. Si aestas est, secretum arboris umbra praebebit; si autumnus, ipsa aeris temperies et strata subter folia locum quietis ostendit. Vere ager floribus depingitur et inter querulas aves psalmi dulcius decantabuntur. Si frigus fuerit et brumales nives, ligna non coemam: calidius vigilabo vel dormiam, certe, quod sciam, vilius non algebo. Habeat sibi Roma suos tumultos, harena saeviat, circus insaniat, theatra luxurient, et quia de nostris dicendum est, matronarum cotidie visitetur senatus: nobis adhaerere Deo bonum est, ponere in domino spem nostram, ut, cum paupertatem istam caelorum regna mutaverint, erumpamus in vocem: 'Quid enim mihi restat in caelo et a te quid volui super terram?' Quo scilicet, cum tanta reppererimus in caelo, parva et caduca quaesisse nos doleamus in terra.

a Cybele so we who, if we were not of the world, would be hated by the world, have a counterfeit mask for every sin to which we are inclined.

Therefore, as today we have traversed a great part of life's journey through rough seas, and as our barque has been now shaken by tempestuous winds, now holed upon rugged rocks, let us take this first chance and make for the haven of a rural retreat. Let us live there on coarse bread and on the green stuff that we water with our own hands, and on milk, country delicacies, cheap and harmless. If thus we spend our days, sleep will not call us away from prayer, nor overfeeding from study. In summer the shade of a tree will give us privacy. In autumn the mild air and the leaves beneath our feet point out a place for rest. In spring the fields are gay with flowers, and the birds' plaintive notes will make our psalms sound all the sweeter. When the cold weather comes with winter's snows, I shall not need to buy wood: whether I keep vigil or lie asleep, I shall be warmer there, and certainly as far as I know, I shall escape the cold at a cheaper rate. Let Rome keep her bustle for herself, the fury of the arena, the madness of the circus, the profligacy of the theatre, and—for I must not forget our Christian friends—the daily meetings of the matrons' senate. For us it is good to cleave to God, and to put our hopes in the Lord, so that, when we have exchanged this poor life for the kingdom of heaven, we may cry aloud: 'Whom have I in heaven but thee? There is none upon earth that I desire beside thee.'[5] Assuredly, when we have found such wealth in heaven, we may well grieve to have sought after poor passing pleasures here on earth.

[5] Psalm lxxiii. 25.

INDEX OF PASSAGES

(with Loeb series number and the date of publication
of available edition)

INDEX